# WJEC Level 1/2 Vocational Award in
# HOSPITALITY & CATERING

**Bev Saunder and Yvonne Mackey**

**HODDER**
EDUCATION
AN HACHETTE UK COMPANY

Hachette UK's policy is to use papers that are natural, renewable and recyclable products and made from wood grown in well-managed forests and other controlled sources. The logging and manufacturing processes are expected to conform to the environmental regulations of the country of origin.

Orders: please contact Hachette UK Distribution, Hely Hutchinson Centre, Milton Road, Didcot, Oxfordshire, OX11 7HH. Telephone: +44 (0)1235 827827. Lines are open from 9 a.m. to 5 p.m., Monday to Friday. Email education@hachette.co.uk. You can also order through our website: www.hoddereducation.co.uk

ISBN: 978 1 3983 6125 6

© Bev Saunder, Yvonne Mackey 2022

First published in 2022 by
Hodder Education,
An Hachette UK Company
Carmelite House
50 Victoria Embankment
London EC4Y 0DZ

www.hoddereducation.co.uk

Impression number    10 9 8 7 6 5 4 3 2

Year        2026  2025  2024  2023

Typeset in India

Produced by DZS Grafik, Printed in Slovenia

A catalogue record for this title is available from the British Library.

# CONTENTS

# Introduction

The hospitality industry is an important sector in the UK economy. It is the third-largest employer in the UK, employing 3.2 million people and contributing approximately £72 billion to the UK economy. It is an exciting, fast-paced industry to work in, made up of a range of different establishments, including hotels, restaurants, pubs, cafés and fast-food outlets, as well as visitor attractions such as theme parks, and sports and music venues. A wide variety of job roles are available in the industry, including chefs, waiting and housekeeping staff, receptionists and managers.

This book has been designed to help you develop the knowledge, understanding and practical skills you'll need to complete the WJEC Level 1/2 Vocational Award in Hospitality and Catering (Technical Award). As well as preparing you for the final exam and controlled assessment, the book will introduce you to the vibrant hospitality and catering industry, and give you an insight into the types of careers available to you in the future, as well as opportunities for further study.

The qualification is made up of two units, both of which are covered in this book, and you must study both of them.

## 1. The hospitality and catering industry

In Unit 1 you will learn about the hospitality and catering industry, including different types of hospitality and catering providers and how they operate, as well as health and safety and food safety in hospitality and catering.

This unit is assessed by a written exam, which is set and marked by WJEC. Your teacher will tell you when you will complete the exam. The exam will last 1 hour 20 minutes and there are 80 marks available; it is worth 40 per cent of your total qualification. The exam will include a mixture of short-answer and extended-response questions based around different hospitality and catering scenarios.

## 2. Hospitality and catering in action

In Unit 2 you will apply your knowledge and understanding of why nutrition is important, and learn how to plan nutritious menus. You will learn a range of practical cooking skills that you will need to prepare, cook and present dishes. You will also learn how to review your own work effectively.

This unit is assessed by a controlled assessment lasting approximately 12 hours and there are 120 marks available; it is worth 60 per cent of your total qualification. Your teacher will give you an assignment brief that has been provided by WJEC; this will include a scenario and details of several tasks that you will need to complete.

# How to use this book

This textbook is divided into two parts, each covering one unit of the WJEC Level 1/2 Vocational Award in Hospitality and Catering specification:

■ Unit 1 The hospitality and catering industry
■ Unit 2 Hospitality and catering in action.

Each of these units is divided into topic areas. All of the teaching content for each learning outcome is covered in the book.

## Key features of the book

The book is organised by the units in the qualification, with each unit broken down into the topic areas covered by the specification. Each unit opener will help you to understand what is covered in the unit, listing the topic areas covered and what you will be assessed on, all fully matched to the requirements of the specification.

### ABOUT THIS UNIT
An introduction to what you will be learning about in each topic.

### TOPICS
The topics are clearly stated so you know exactly what is covered.

### HOW WILL I BE ASSESSED?
Assessment methods are clearly listed and fully mapped to the specification.

### What will I learn?
A summary of the knowledge and understanding that you will be covering.

### Getting started
Short activities to introduce you to the topic.

### Key terms

Important terms highlighted to aid understanding.

# Unit 1 The hospitality and catering industry

## ABOUT THIS UNIT

In this unit you will study the hospitality and catering industry. You will learn about:

- the different types of providers in the hospitality and catering industry, and how they operate
- the job roles that are available, what it is like to work in the industry, and the skills,

qualifications and experience needed for each of these jobs

- what makes a successful hospitality or catering business
- health and safety and food safety requirements in hospitality and catering.

## TOPICS

The topics covered in this unit are:

1.1 Hospitality and catering provision
1.2 How hospitality and catering providers operate
1.3 Health and safety in hospitality and catering
1.4 Food safety in hospitality and catering

## HOW WILL I BE ASSESSED?

You will be assessed by a written examination, which contributes towards 40 per cent of the qualification.

The exam lasts 1 hour 20 minutes and is worth 80 marks.

There will be a range of short- and extended-answer questions based around applied situations. Some questions will include stimulus material, such as a photo, table or graph, which you will need to respond to.

# 1.1 Hospitality and catering provision

**What will I learn?**

In this topic you will gain knowledge and understanding of the following areas:

1.1.1  Hospitality and catering providers
1.1.2  Working in the hospitality and catering industry
1.1.3  Working conditions in the hospitality and catering industry
1.1.4  Contributing factors to the success of hospitality and catering provision

## Getting started

1  What do you think the term 'commercial non-residential' means?
2  What types of food and drink would be served by the following commercial non-residential providers?
   – Cruise ship               – Street-food truck
   – Café                      – Public house
   – Coffee shop               – Takeaway
   – Fast-food outlet          – Vending machine

## 1.1.1 Hospitality and catering providers

**Key terms**

**Hospitality** providing accommodation, food and drinks in a variety of places outside the home

**Catering** providing food and drink services to customers

**Beverage** a drink other than water

The **hospitality** and **catering** industry provides people with accommodation, food and **beverages** outside of the home. There are two different types of hospitality and catering provider:

1  commercial establishments, which are businesses that provide food and drink services and operate to make a profit
2  non-commercial providers, which do not need to make a profit.

We will look at each of these in turn.

There are two types of commercial establishment:

1  residential – businesses that provide accommodation as well as catering and hospitality
2  non-residential – businesses that provide catering and hospitality services, but not accommodation.

▲ **A hotel lobby**

# Commercial (residential)

## B&Bs

A bed and breakfast (B&B for short) is an establishment that offers overnight accommodation and breakfast. B&Bs are often private family homes where rooms are made available to guests. The rooms either have en-suite bathrooms or use of a shared bathroom. Breakfast is usually served in a dining room or the owner's kitchen.

## Guest houses

A guest house is generally a larger property, with more than five bedrooms. It is more like a small, privately owned hotel. Breakfast is served in the morning. Other meals, such as dinner, are often available. Larger guest houses have **communal** areas such as a lounge and dining room. Communal means an area shared by a number of people, for example a lounge or dining room would be communal as they are available for all guests to use. Some have a licensed bar.

> **Key term**
>
> **Communal** shared, for example a communal kitchen

## Airbnb

Airbnb is an online marketplace that people can use to rent out all or part of their residential property. The owner – a 'host' – rents out a room or an entire property on a short-term basis to people who need accommodation – 'guests'. Simple breakfast ingredients are sometimes provided for guests to use, such as cereals, eggs, bread and croissants.

Airbnb is extremely popular as a way of making money as a host; and for guests the rooms or properties can prove very cost effective at extremely competitive prices.

## Campsites and caravan parks

Many camping and caravan sites are designed so that people can bring their own tents or caravans and choose a pitch. There are many sites all over the UK, which are usually well equipped with a range of facilities including electricity hook-ups, toilets, showers and cafés. Some sites also have static caravans and tents that can be rented.

## Holiday parks, lodges, pods and cabins

Holiday parks, such as Center Parcs, offer leisure and hospitality facilities aimed at families. Many have swimming pools, nature walks, spas, and outdoor sports and activities on offer. They have a range of different restaurants, takeaways, bars and coffee shops. These parks offer many indoor activities also so that people can holiday at them all year round.

Holiday parks offer different types of accommodation to suit different budgets, such as lodges, pods and cabins.

Lodges are modern holiday homes that are often built to residential standards. They are at the top end of the market, with facilities such as hot tubs, and are designed for those wanting home comforts.

Pods offer the cheaper option of a glamping experience. **Glamping** is a blend of the words 'glamorous' and 'camping', and is camping that offers more luxurious facilities than traditional camping. Pods provide shelter for year-round camping and are designed to keep people warm and dry, even in poor weather. Camping pods vary in terms of the facilities offered, with some having beds, electricity, a compact kitchen area and even a hot tub.

▲ **Camping pods**

▲ **A log cabin**

Cabins are holiday homes made from wood. The wood used can be of different thicknesses, making some suitable for use only in the warmer months of the year. Cabins are often placed in woodland areas of holiday parks, but they can also be found as stand-alone holiday lets.

## Hotels

Hotels are establishments that provide overnight accommodation and food and drink options. The bedrooms usually have en-suite bathrooms. Hotels are graded according to the facilities they offer, such as:

- breakfast
- evening meals
- bar snacks
- lunch
- **room service**
- laundry
- spa, gym, swimming pool.

A fast-growing market is budget hotels, such as Travelodge. These simply offer accommodation, with an option to include breakfast, which is charged for separately.

## Activity

Research the facilities, standards and cost per night of different styles of hotels in your local area.

You could present your findings in a table like this:

| Hotel | Cost per night | Meals offered with cost | Extra facilities available |
|---|---|---|---|
|  |  |  |  |
|  |  |  |  |
|  |  |  |  |

### Extension activity

Choose one hotel and write a review that would be suitable for a platform such as Tripadvisor.

# Motels

Motels are roadside hotels designed primarily for motorists. They can be found alongside motorways and A roads. They tend to focus on business people who need an overnight stay, or people who are travelling long distances and wish to break up their journey. They are usually reasonably priced, consisting of an en-suite room with basic services such as TV, and tea- and coffee-making facilities. There is not always a restaurant on-site but there are often places nearby where food and beverages can be purchased.

# Hostels

Hostels are designed for those who are looking for accommodation to suit a limited budget. They offer a range of rooms: from single, twin or family to low-cost dormitory-style rooms. The focus is on travellers sharing a social experience, so they have communal kitchens and lounges. There are also shared bathrooms, although some higher-priced bedrooms do have an en-suite. Most will also have laundry facilities.

# Cruise ships

Cruising is a popular leisure activity. Cruise ships are like floating hotels and offer a whole range of on-board facilities. Guest accommodation is in cabins – these usually range from basic inside cabins to those with sea views and balconies or luxury suites. On luxury cruises in particular, the standard, quality and range of food offered is extremely important, with dining often being an important selling point. In general, cruise ships have a main dining room where you can sit down and order from a menu. These are large, banquet-style restaurants where there is a dress code and you share a table with others. In addition, there is always a choice of speciality restaurants in smaller venues where you can have your own table. Very often these restaurants are themed, such as steakhouses, French bistros or Italian trattorias. Many cruise ships have some form of food available all day and night.

# Commercial (non-residential)

## Airlines

Budget airlines do not always include food and drink as part of the cost of the ticket. Instead, passengers can choose and pay for food and beverages from a menu on the plane. A range of hot and cold drinks is usually offered, along with a selection of snacks, sandwiches, sweets and chocolates served from a trolley. In-flight hot meals, such as a cooked breakfast or dinner, are usually ordered and paid for when you book your ticket and then become part of the ticket price.

On long-haul flights with premium airlines, meals are usually included as part of the ticket price. Airline meals are generally prepared on the ground in catering facilities close to the airport. They are then transported on to the plane and stored in refrigerators for flight attendants to prepare and serve to passengers during the flight.

▲ **Many airlines serve food and drinks from trolleys**

## Long-distance trains

Long-distance trains sometimes have a dining carriage that you can go to for a sit-down meal, or a buffet car where you can order hot and cold drinks and a variety of hot and cold snacks, sandwiches, cakes and so on.

Trains may also have mobile food and drinks trolleys that are brought down the aisles throughout the journey, serving snacks and hot and cold drinks.

## Tea rooms

A tea room is an establishment that serves tea and other light refreshments. It may be a room set aside in a hotel that serves afternoon tea. Afternoon tea is also popular in tea rooms, and is usually served between 2 and 4 p.m. An afternoon tea menu usually consists of a pot of tea with a selection of small sandwiches, pastries and cakes.

# Cafés and coffee shops

A café is a small eating and drinking establishment very similar to a coffee shop. Cafés tend to offer a wider range of food than coffee shops however, in the form of light refreshments and light meals. They sometimes offer table service.

Coffee shops have been a rapidly growing market, made up of both well-known chains, such as Starbucks, Costa and Caffè Nero, and independent coffee shops. Coffee shops provide a variety of coffees, other beverages and snacks. They have seating areas for those wanting to eat and drink in, but also offer a takeaway service. They tend not to offer table service, requiring customers to order at a counter and take their food and/or drink on a tray to a table.

▲ **A coffee shop**

# Fast-food outlets

Fast-food outlets offer food that is made to order quickly and can be taken away from the restaurant or stall to eat elsewhere, although seats and tables are often provided too. There is very little waiting time. One example of a fast-food outlet is McDonald's.

▲ **A fast-food outlet**

## Food provided by stadia, concert halls and tourist attractions

Food is usually available at stadia, concert halls and tourist attractions. Depending on the type of venue, there may be a range of providers present, including coffee shops, burger bars, pubs serving food, and bakery products available to buy such as pies, pasties, sausage rolls, cakes and sandwiches. There may be options to sit down and eat, or to order and collect a drink or snack while on the move. Some tourist attractions, such as National Trust properties, have their own cafés, tea rooms and restaurants.

## Mobile food vans and street-food trucks

▲ **Street food**

Street food is ready-to-eat food or drink sold in a street or public place, such as at a market or festival. It is often sold from a portable stall or mobile food van where the food is prepared in front of you and is designed to be eaten immediately. Some stalls have seating available.

### Activity

1 Find out more about street food by searching YouTube for the clips entitled 'street food UK' by the Nationwide Caterers Association, and '5 of the best street food finds in London' by Great Big Story. Then visit the website www.streetfood.org.uk.
2 Write a report on your findings.

In your report use these subheadings:
- The range of companies offering street food
- The range of food sold, menu prices and whether they cater for special dietary needs
- Their unique selling points

### Extension activity

If you were setting up your own street-food stall, what would you cook and serve, and why?

## Pop-up restaurants

If a restaurant is in operation for a only short period of time then it is referred to as a pop-up restaurant. They often appear at venues such as festivals, or at a particular time of year, for example Christmas. Sometimes they take over a location on a short-term let, which enables them to test the market before committing fully to the restaurant business.

## Public houses and bars

Public houses (pubs) are premises that have a licence to sell alcohol. There are very few pubs that only serve alcoholic and non-alcoholic drinks, with most serving food too. Some have diversified further and have introduced entertainment such as live music, quizzes and large TV screens showing major sporting events.

Bars are set up as selling points for alcoholic and non-alcoholic beverages, and can often be found at wedding venues and events such as festivals.

## Restaurants and bistros

In a formal restaurant, food is usually served to customers by waiting staff. It can be served in one of two ways:

1  plate – the meal ordered is plated up and brought to the customer's table by a waiter
2  waiting service – the food is served to the customer at the table by staff.

There are many different restaurants in the UK. Often the food they serve is based on a particular country's cuisine – Bella Italia, for example, is an Italian restaurant chain.

A bistro is a small, informal restaurant with a casual setting. Prices are generally cheaper than in a formal restaurant. Bistros originated in France.

▲ **A formal restaurant**

## Takeaways

Takeaway restaurants either take an order and then deliver the food to a customer's home, or the customer can go to the takeaway in person, order the food they want and take it away.

## Vending machines

In automatic vending, drink and snack items are stored in a machine and can be selected by the customer. Vending machines are often sited in establishments where it may not always be possible to get access to food (for example colleges and hospitals). Some farm shops operate vending machines that are accessible at any time, selling produce such as fresh milk, cheese and eggs.

▲ **A vending machine**

### Activity

Write a review of somewhere you have been to eat out.

Use these subheadings to help you:
- Type of service
- Quality of service
- Menu choices and prices
- Options for special dietary needs
- Quality of food eaten
- Presentation of food
- Layout of restaurant
- Value for money
- Portion size

### Extension activity

Discuss the type of service. Would you recommend it? Why, or why not?

# Non-commercial (residential)

## Armed forces

The British armed forces are made up of the Army, Royal Navy and Royal Air Force. Catering for the armed forces is very specialised. The armed forces recruit and train chefs who have to deliver the necessary supplies and prepare meals in a variety of locations. These include **barracks** (the group of buildings where they live), the **mess** (an area where they eat and socialise) and **in the field** (away from base camp).

## Boarding schools

Catering is important at boarding schools because all meals are provided for the students who live in. A boarding school will have a dining hall where **boarders** can socialise, as they usually eat together. Boarders are provided with breakfast, lunch and dinner, and care needs to be taken to provide them with high-quality, nutritious meals.

## Colleges and university residences

Some colleges and universities offer the option of self-catering accommodation. Self-catering residences will have a communal kitchen that is shared by a number of students. Colleges and university residences usually have the option of catered accommodation also. This would usually be a package consisting of breakfast and lunch or dinner, offered every day during term time. Schools, colleges and universities also often have hospitality and catering provision for non-residents (see the section titled 'Schools, colleges and universities' in the information about non-commercial (non-residential) establishments, below).

## Hospitals, hospices and care homes

In hospitals, hospices and care homes, food is an essential part of patient care. Food served should be of good quality so that it gives a patient or resident the nutrients they need, especially if they are recovering from illness or injury. In many hospitals a dietician works with the catering team and the individual patient to discuss the most beneficial meal plan and specific dietary requirements.

## Prisons

Prison catering is either run by contract caterers or by the prison service. The food is prepared and served within the prison by caterers supported by prisoners. In addition, there are staff food service facilities for those who work in the prison.

▲ **Food served in hospitals is an essential part of patient care**

> **Key terms**
>
> **Barracks** where people in the armed forces live
>
> **Mess** an area where people in the armed forces eat and socialise
>
> **In the field** when members of the armed forces are away from their base camp
>
> **Boarders** students who live in school during term time

# Non-commercial (non-residential)

## Canteens in working establishments (subsidised)

Canteens are where food and drink are provided for a workforce in a dining room-style setting. Workers buy their food and drink at a subsidised rate; this means that they purchase it at a price lower than its actual cost and the difference is made up by the employer.

Many companies are cutting costs, which means that fewer workplaces now offer this service to their staff. In 2015, 47 per cent of workplaces had a canteen, down from 56 per cent in 2010, 66 per cent in 2000 and 82 per cent in 1995 (*source*: **www.lrdpublications.org.uk/publications.php?pub=WR&iss=1758&id=idp10120192**).

## Charity-run food providers

The Trussell Trust manages a network of more than 1200 food bank centres. The public donate non-perishable, in-date food at places such as schools, churches and supermarket collection points, which is then sorted into food parcels to be given to people who need them.

Care professionals such as social workers can issue a food bank voucher to those in need. This can then be exchanged for a food bank parcel that consists of three days' worth of nutritionally balanced, non-perishable food from their local food bank.

Other food charities in the UK include FareShare and Feeding Britain, which also provide food to those who need it.

▲ **A food bank**

### Activity

The Trussell Trust is responsible for food banks. Look at **www.trusselltrust.org** and answer these questions on food banks:

1 How do food banks help food poverty?
2 Which people are helped by food banks?
3 How many people benefit from food banks?
4 How much food is donated?
5 What is a standard food bank shopping list?

### Extension activity

Write a report on the role of the Trussell Trust.

## Meals on wheels

'Get meals at home' (also known as 'meals on wheels') delivers meals to individuals in their homes, if they are eligible. To be eligible, a person must be over 55 years old, or aged between 18 and 54 and have dementia, a learning disability or a physical disability. The service is funded partly by government and partly by donations, with the meals delivered by volunteers. Depending on a person's circumstances, meals are either free or a nominal amount is charged. Meals are balanced, including a protein, a starchy food, vegetables, dessert, and milk or juice.

## Schools, colleges and universities

On a university or college campus, there will be a range of outlets from which food and drinks can be purchased, such as restaurants, cafés and coffee shops.

Secondary schools usually offer a range of food and other refreshments, starting before school hours and then throughout the school day, to cater flexibly for all students' needs. There is usually a 'grab and go' facility, providing freshly prepared hot and cold food at break times and often before school. There is usually a seated dining hall offering hot and cold plated food at lunchtime. There is also always the alternative of students bringing in their own packed lunches and snacks.

Primary schools usually have an external caterer who will come in with hot meals at lunchtime; these are ordered and paid for in advance. Alternatively, packed lunches can be brought in by students.

## Food service

There are many ways in which food can be served, including at a table, at a counter or directly to a person.

▲ **Plate service**

▲ **A café**

Table 1.1 **Types of table service**

| Type of table service | Description |
|---|---|
| Banquet | Banquets are formal sit-down meals, usually involving a large number of people, often for a special event such as a wedding. |
| Family-style | Dishes are put on the table with serving spoons and customers help themselves. |
| Gueridon (trolley or movable service) | Food is served from a side table or a trolley; sometimes the customer's food is cooked at the table, usually for dramatic effect, for example in the case of flambéed steaks and crêpes. |
| Plate service | The meal is plated up in the kitchen and brought to the customer's table by waiting staff. |
| Silver service | A waiter uses a spoon and fork held in one hand to transfer food from a serving dish to the customer's plate; full silver service is where all the food is served this way. |

Table 1.2 **Types of counter service**

| Type of counter service | Description |
|---|---|
| Buffet | A selection of dishes is laid out on a table or counter for the customers to help themselves. There are different styles of buffets:<br>■ sit-down buffet – the customer selects the food they want and then sits down to eat; the tables are usually set in the same way as in any restaurant where food is served to the customer<br>■ stand-up or fork buffet – the customer selects food and then eats it while standing; the food should be easy to eat either without cutlery or with just a fork<br>■ finger buffet – the customer selects food and then sits down to eat it; the food is designed to be eaten without cutlery and is often small bites, such as sandwiches and canapés. |
| Cafeteria | A menu is displayed and customers walk past food counters selecting the items they want; they pay for the food before they eat it, and can then collect cutlery and condiments before sitting down to eat. |
| Fast food | A takeaway service where it is possible to eat in or take away; there is usually a limited menu to allow the food to be cooked quickly; the food is ordered and collected from a counter. |

**Table 1.3 Types of personal service**

| Type of personal service | Description |
|---|---|
| Home delivery | A large number of catering establishments offer home delivery within a certain radius. There are two ways of doing this. A customer can contact the establishment direct and order food to be delivered, or order through a company such as Just Eat or Deliveroo, which will deliver to the door. These companies' services are usually accessed online or via an app. |
| Takeaway restaurants | The restaurant will take an order via telephone, internet or in person. Examples include Chinese, Indian and Italian takeaways. Customers can go to the takeaway in person to order and then take the food away to eat it. |
| Tray or trolley | This is where food and drink are served to people on a tray. Trays are used on aeroplanes, in hospitals or in room service at a hotel. Sometimes the food is served from a trolley. Trolleys are used on trains and aeroplanes, and in offices. |
| Vending machine | Has a glass front and drinks and snacks are stored inside. People select and pay for what they want then take it away with them to consume. |

# Residential service

When booking an overnight stay, it is necessary to decide which of the following residential services is wanted or needed.

## Rooms

There are different types of rooms to choose from:

- single – a room for one person
- double – a room for two people; may have one or more beds
- king – a room with a king-sized bed; may be occupied by one or more people
- suite – where there is a living room area as well as a bedroom area
- family room – the room is larger than a standard room and can usually accommodate four to six people; it has either extra twin beds or a bed settee
- en-suite bath/shower room – the room has its own private bathroom consisting of toilet, wash basin, and either a bath, shower over bath or shower
- shared facilities – a private room to sleep in but bathroom facilities shared with other people staying at the accommodation.

▲ **A hotel bedroom**

# Refreshments

The refreshments served at residential accommodation will depend on the type of accommodation being provided.

## Breakfast

Several different breakfast options are possible:

- light breakfast – either cereals, yoghurt and fruit, porridge or toast and a hot drink
- continental breakfast – rolls, brioche, pain au chocolat, pain au raisin or croissants, jams and coffee; sometimes cheese and cold meat, such as ham or salami, are served
- full English breakfast – can include eggs, bacon, sausages, baked beans, tomatoes, black pudding and mushrooms; it is also eaten with toast and tea.

## Lunch

Some accommodation will provide lunch that can be eaten in the dining area. Most will provide food that can be purchased at lunchtime. This can be in the form of hot and cold snacks, hot and cold drinks, and sandwiches.

## Evening meal

Some types of residential accommodation offer a range of menu items. These can vary from a three-course meal in their own restaurant to a more informal meal in a bar area.

## 24-hour room service/restaurant

This is a service where guests can choose items of food and drink and have them delivered to their room at any time of the day or night. Some residential accommodation has a restaurant that will close in the evening, but a bar area where light meals can be ordered until late into the evening.

# Conference and function facilities

Functions can take many different forms, for example conferences, formal dinners, meetings, training events and shows. A **conference** is an event where people meet to discuss a particular topic, or come together for some training. At a conference or a function, food and drink is usually provided. The type of food and drink provided will depend on the market being catered for. It could take the form of beverages, pastries and biscuits served mid-morning, a hot or cold lunch, and beverages again in the afternoon.

# Leisure facilities

**Key term**

**Conference** an event where people meet to discuss a particular topic or come together for some training

▲ **Leisure facilities at a hotel**

## 1.1 Hospitality and catering provision

It is common for high-end accommodation such as hotels to offer a range of leisure facilities, for example a:

- spa – where guests can have beauty treatments and massages; there may also be amenities such as small relaxation pools, jacuzzis and saunas
- gym – where guests can use a variety of gym equipment such as running machines, rowing machines and weights, often under the supervision of trainers
- swimming pool – these vary in size and are used for both fitness and leisure.

# Hotel and guest house standards (star ratings)

Hotels and guest houses are often given a star rating. These star ratings help customers to know what services and facilities they can expect at a hotel or guest house. The quality of the services provided is rated on a scale from one to five stars. Table 1.4 lists details of the requirements for different star ratings.

**Table 1.4 Hotel star ratings**

| Star rating | Requirements to meet this standard |
|---|---|
| ★ | At least five bedrooms with en-suite facilities<br>Open seven days a week<br>Guests have access at all times<br>Reception area<br>Restaurant serving breakfast seven days a week and evening meals five days a week<br>Licensed bar |
| ★ ★ | The requirements for one star, plus higher standards of cleanliness, maintenance and hospitality |
| ★ ★ ★ | Access without a key from 7 a.m. to 11 p.m. and with key after 11 p.m.<br>Dinner served six evenings a week, with snacks on the seventh<br>Room service for drinks and snacks during the day and evening<br>En-suite facilities<br>Internal telephone system<br>Wi-Fi in public areas |
| ★ ★ ★ ★ | 24-hour room service<br>Restaurant open for breakfast and dinner seven days a week<br>Wi-Fi in room<br>24-hour access and on-duty staff<br>En-suite facilities<br>Enhanced facilities, for example afternoon tea<br>Higher staffing levels |
| ★ ★ ★ ★ ★ | Open all year round<br>Proactive service and customer care<br>Multilingual receptionists<br>Other facilities, such as a spa or business centre (a room in a hotel with facilities such as computers, desks, Wi-Fi and printers; this allows guests to work while they are staying at the hotel)<br>Enhanced services, for example concierge, valet parking<br>Restaurant open every day for all meals<br>En-suite facilities; 80 per cent of rooms have a bath and shower |

# Restaurant standards

The three main restaurant rating systems used in the UK are:

1. Michelin stars
2. AA Rosette Awards
3. The Good Food Guide reviews.

Michelin stars are a rating system used to grade restaurants on their quality. Stars are awarded to restaurants judged to be of a particularly high standard. The judging criteria are the same for each restaurant, focusing on the quality of the ingredients, cooking techniques and taste, so stars are awarded solely on the standard of the cuisine:

- one star is a very good restaurant
- two stars is excellent cooking
- three stars is exceptional cuisine.

AA Rosette Awards score restaurants from one to five:

- one rosette – food is prepared with care, understanding and skill, using good-quality ingredients
- two rosettes – excellent restaurants that demonstrate greater precision in cooking; there will be obvious attention to the selection of quality ingredients
- three rosettes – outstanding restaurants where there is selection of the highest-quality ingredients; timing, seasoning and the judgement of flavour combinations will be consistently excellent
- four rosettes – these restaurants demonstrate superb technical skills and consistency
- five rosettes – the cooking at these restaurants compares with the best in the world; they demonstrate breathtaking culinary skills.

*Source*: **www.theaa.com/hotel-services/ratings-and-awards**

The Good Food Guide is an annual guide to the best restaurants in the UK. It gives restaurants a score from 1 (capable cooking but some inconsistencies) to 10 (perfection).

Up until 2020 The Good Food Guide was available to buy as a printed book. However, it is likely that future updates will be online.

## Knowledge check

1. What is a residential commercial establishment?
2. What is a B&B?
3. State two advantages of staying in a hostel.
4. Describe what is meant by afternoon tea.
5. What is a bistro?
6. Describe how a food bank operates.
7. Give a definition of silver service.
8. Which would be the most suitable type of room in a hotel for a family of two parents and two children?
9. State three items that could be included in a continental breakfast.
10. If a restaurant has been awarded three rosettes, what does this mean?

## Case study

Airbnb was founded by three Americans, who developed the business in 2008. They used their own house as a bed and breakfast to make some extra money to pay their rent when they realised that a big conference was coming to their area and all the hotels were fully booked. They initially used airbeds, hence its original name: AirBed & Breakfast. In 2009 they received some extra investment and changed the name of the business to Airbnb.

Airbnb is considered to be part of the 'sharing economy'. It acts as a go-between, putting people wanting to rent out rooms or houses in touch with those who are looking for accommodation.

As a guest, it offers you someone's home or a room in their home as a place to stay. It is a great way to find a place if you are travelling, would like to explore a location, or want something different from a hotel or bed and breakfast.

As a host, it offers you the chance to rent out space in your home, or your entire home, and make some money.

### Questions

1 Describe how Airbnb works.
2 Why do you think Airbnb is popular with travellers?
3 Summarise the advantages and disadvantages of using Airbnb.
4 If you were to include a welcome hamper in your Airbnb accommodation, what items of food and drink would you include?

## 1.1.2 Working in the hospitality and catering industry

There are a range of employment opportunities within the hospitality and catering industry.

▲ **A hospitality workforce, including serving staff, management and kitchen staff**

## Front of house

The **front of house** is the part of the hospitality and catering business where employees have direct face-to-face contact with customers.

### Front-of-house manager

Front-of-house managers are responsible for making sure that front-of-house staff have the necessary training and complete their duties to a high standard. They also ensure that good customer service is provided.

### Head waiter/maître d'hôtel

A head waiter/maître d'hôtel manages the food service section. They will welcome guests and oversee the waiting staff to ensure excellent customer service. They will organise staff duty rotas and, in busy times, take on the duties of waiting staff.

### Waiting staff

Waiting staff prepare tables, give out menus, take orders, serve food, clear tables and take payment from customers.

# Concierge

A concierge assists hotel guests by making reservations, booking taxis, and booking tickets for local attractions and events.

# Receptionist

Receptionists are responsible for meeting customers and directing them to the correct person or place. They check customers in and manage booking systems, for example for a restaurant.

# Valets

A valet will meet and greet guests when they arrive, and park and collect their vehicles.

# Housekeeping

## Chambermaid

Chambermaids or room attendants clean and prepare rooms for guests, changing towels and bedding.

## Cleaner

Cleaners are needed in all areas of hospitality and catering. They carry out the necessary cleaning tasks, such as dusting, vacuuming, mopping floors and wiping surfaces.

## Maintenance

Maintenance staff complete any repairs that can be done in-house and book outside professionals, such as gas engineers or lift repair technicians, to carry out more specialist jobs.

## Caretaker

A caretaker usually works within the maintenance team and is responsible for maintaining the building and its grounds. They will also work alongside contractors such as electricians, gas engineers and plumbers.

**Activity**

There are a range of employment opportunities in hospitality and catering. Identify the employment opportunities in:
1 front of house
2 housekeeping.

**Extension activity**

Choose three employment opportunities in front of house and three in housekeeping, and explain what each role involves.

# Kitchen brigade

The **kitchen brigade** is a team of people who work in the kitchen. Each of them will have a clear role.

▲ **A chef working in a kitchen**

## Executive chef

The executive chef, or head chef, is in charge of the kitchen. This job involves menu planning, food production, ordering food from suppliers, costing dishes, managing stock, kitchen hygiene, planning staff rotas, and recruiting and training staff.

## Sous-chef

The sous-chef is directly in charge of food production and often also in charge of the day-to-day running of the kitchen. Most sous-chefs start off as a commis chef, then become a chef de partie.

## Chef de partie

The chef de partie (section chef) has responsibility for a particular section of the menu or area of the kitchen, and a varying number of staff to whom they allocate tasks. The jobs to be carried out vary from one establishment to another depending on the head chef's organisation and the size of the establishment. Most large establishments could have chefs de partie in the following areas:

- sauce chefs
- pastry chefs
- fish chefs
- roast chefs

- vegetable chefs
- soup chefs
- larder chefs – these chefs prepare cold starters and salads
- relief chefs – chefs who can be called on if another chef is unable to come to work.

## Commis chef

The commis chef, or assistant chef, does the easier tasks, such as checking stock and collecting and measuring ingredients. They may be part of an apprenticeship scheme or studying at college.

## Pastry chef

These chefs make breads, pastries, cakes, confectionery, batters, desserts and other baked goods.

## Kitchen assistant

A kitchen assistant supports a chef de partie by cleaning, washing up, sorting and storing ingredients, and helping with the preparation of food.

### Activity

Choose three of the following chef de partie roles:

- sauce chef
- pastry chef
- fish chef
- roast chef
- vegetable chef
- soup chef
- larder chef

Explain what types of dishes each of these would be expected to prepare and make.

### Extension activity

Using the website **www.caterer.com** write a job description for three of the above chef de partie roles.

## Apprentice

An apprentice will work alongside a member of the kitchen brigade, who will train them 'on the job', helping them to gain knowledge and experience of the role. Information on apprenticeships can be found on page 26.

## Kitchen porter/plongeur

The kitchen porter, or plongeur, washes up and may also do some basic vegetable preparation.

# Management

## Food and beverage

A food and beverage manager will be responsible for managing the food and beverage team. They will oversee the reservations, monitor and pay bills, and ensure their staff are well trained at carrying out their duties.

## Housekeeping

The head housekeeper allocates jobs to room attendants and ensures that rooms are cleaned correctly. They must communicate well with reception to know which rooms need cleaning and inform them once the rooms are ready for the guests.

## Marketing

A marketing manager is responsible for promoting the business. They are responsible for managing the website, emails, social media and any advertising to ensure the business is successful, new customers are attracted and existing customers return.

# Personal attributes

A **personal attribute** is a quality or a characteristic that a person has. Employers will be looking for a specific set of attributes in their employees; Table 1.5 lists and describes some of these.

> **Key term**
>
> **Personal attribute**
> a quality or
> characteristic that a
> person has

▲ **A waiter demonstrating good customer service**

> **Activity**
>
> Imagine you are writing your CV, as you want to work in hospitality and catering.
> 1  Describe your personal attributes.
> 2  Which role do you think you would be best suited to?

## Table 1.5 **Personal attributes**

| Personal attribute | Description |
|---|---|
| Organised | Being organised means that you are able to carry out your responsibilities in a logical and efficient way. |
| Hard-working | Working in the hospitality and catering industry often means working long and unsociable hours. Some roles require you to be on your feet for long periods of time. This means you need to be hard-working and able to demonstrate that you can work energetically and conscientiously to ensure your job is completed to the necessary high standards. |
| Punctual | When you are punctual it means that you will arrive at work at the correct time or you will complete the tasks allocated to you within an agreed time frame. |
| Hygienic | When providing a service to others, it is essential that you have high standards of personal hygiene – your body should be clean, and your clothes or uniform should be clean and tidy. |
| Pleasant | Customer service is of the highest importance, so it is crucial to be polite and well mannered. A genuine smile demonstrates how pleasant you are, and is appreciated in customer service. |
| Calm | It is inevitable when working in the catering and hospitality industry that you will come across difficult situations. Getting food cooked and delivered efficiently can be stressful. You may have to deal with complaints from aggressive customers. Keeping calm and not losing your temper in these situations is crucial. Keeping calm means that you do not show any signs of worry or anger in difficult circumstances. |
| Friendly | Being friendly is also an important part of customer service. It means being kind, pleasant and helpful towards others. |
| Good communicator | This skill involves how well you can communicate with other people – verbally, non-verbally and in written form. Showing that you are actively listening is an important skill because it means that you can use your body language (for example nodding) to show people that you are listening carefully to what they are saying so you can respond in the best way. |
| Team player | This skill refers to how well you work with others within a group of people. You will need to work with others as a team when tasks need sharing or problems need resolving. |
| Good people skills | This skill means communicating with others in your team, or with customers, in an effective way. |
| Willingness to learn and develop | This means you are always prepared to learn new skills or knowledge, and to continue developing skills and knowledge to achieve either your personal goals or goals within your role. It is also important to be aware of any new ideas and trends that would help your work performance. |
| Flexible | Being flexible means you are comfortable if things change – you can adapt to and work with any changes to routine. |

# Qualifications and experience

▲ **Training to be a chef**

The qualifications you have and the experience you gain while working in the industry will have an impact on the salary you could earn. Executive chefs will have worked their way up through the kitchen brigade. In order to progress in the catering industry, they would need to gain experience as a commis chef, then progress to the role of chef de partie (for example, as a pastry chef), then sous-chef and, finally, executive chef. The same applies to front-of-house staff; a room attendant would gain experience to become a housekeeper.

Apprenticeships and colleges usually require five good GCSE passes, although the entry requirements may be lower for some Level 1 courses. This could be followed by a qualification such as a diploma or certificate.

## Apprenticeships

> **Key term**
>
> **Apprenticeship** a combination of on-the-job training and classroom learning

Many of the jobs within the catering industry can be accessed via an **apprenticeship**. This means you train for a job while you are working. In some cases, you may also attend college on a part-time basis. Apprenticeships combine practical on-the-job training with study. They take between one and five years to complete.

As an apprentice, you will:

- earn wages, including holiday pay
- work with experienced staff
- have a mentor to support you
- learn new skills needed for the job
- study for a related qualification (possibly on day release).

Apprenticeships are for people aged 16 or above, living in the UK and not in full-time education. You can apply for an apprenticeship while you are still at school.

**Table 1.6 Different levels of apprenticeship**

| Name | Equivalent educational level | Level |
|---|---|---|
| Intermediate | Five GCSEs at grades 9 to 4 | 2 |
| Advanced | Two A level passes | 3 |
| Higher | Foundation degree and above | 4, 5, 6 and 7 |
| Degree | Bachelor's or master's degree | 6 and 7 |

*Source*: **www.gov.uk/become-apprentice**

# Experience in the role/sector

At certain times of the year there is increased demand for staff in the hospitality and catering industry. Demand increases during the summer when, for example, festivals are very popular and offer opportunities for catering businesses such as street-food trucks. Eating and drinking out is a popular leisure activity, even more so during the summer holiday period. Working during this busy time offers a valuable way to develop your skills should you wish to work in the hospitality and catering industry.

There are part-time jobs available in the hospitality and catering industry, particularly at weekends and lunchtimes, and in the evenings. These hours may suit people who have to work around young children, or someone at college/university who either wants experience or needs some extra money.

# Relevant school, college and/or university qualifications

Many different training opportunities are available to those wanting to pursue a career in hospitality and catering.

**Table 1.7 Training opportunities in hospitality and catering**

| Level | Type of training |
|---|---|
| Key stage 4 school courses | Level 1/2 Vocational Award in Hospitality and Catering |
| Post-16 to 19 | Colleges offer many courses for those leaving school after Year 11, for example:<br>■ Certificate in Hospitality and Catering Level 1<br>■ Certificate in Introduction to Culinary Skills Level 1<br>■ Diploma in Introduction to Professional Cookery Level 1<br>■ Diploma in Hospitality and Catering Level 2<br>■ Diploma in Professional Cookery Level 2 |
| Universities | Universities offer degree, HND and HNC courses in subjects such as:<br>■ catering<br>■ hospitality<br>■ culinary arts<br>■ hotel management<br>■ food and beverage service |

# Knowledge check

1 Name two members of staff who would be front of house.
2 Name two different types of chef.
3 List three responsibilities of an executive chef.
4 Why is being hard-working such a useful attribute if you work in the hospitality and catering industry?
5 State two advantages of doing an apprenticeship.

## Activity

Different job roles require different personal attributes. For example, a housekeeper needs to be calm, friendly, pleasant, a good communicator and able to work in a team.

List three attributes that would be useful for each of these job roles:

1 head waiter
2 concierge
3 executive chef
4 cleaner
5 marketing manager.

### Extension activity

Imagine you are applying for one of the jobs above. Write a letter of application stating why you would be suitable for the job (think about personal attributes).

## Case study

Nando's is a dining restaurant chain that was founded in Johannesburg, South Africa, in 1987. It has a Mozambican/Portuguese theme.

An engineer called Fernando Duarte took his friend to a Portuguese takeaway called Chickenland for a meal. After tasting its chicken cooked in peri-peri sauce, they liked it so much that they bought the restaurant for the equivalent of £25,000. They renamed the restaurant Nando's after Fernando.

In 2020, Nando's had 958 restaurants around the world (*source*: www.statista.com/statistics/953079/nando-s-restaurant-numbers/).

Nando's specialises in flame-grilled chicken dishes with peri-peri marinades ranging from medium and hot to extra hot and extra extra hot.

It opened its first UK restaurant in London in 1992. Initially the business struggled as it focused just on takeaway trade, but the growth of the restaurant trade made the business very successful due to its excellent teamwork and customer service.

### Questions

1 What different job roles are available at Nando's?
2 Describe how Nando's staff work as a team.
3 What do the staff do at Nando's to ensure excellent customer service?

Use the following websites to help you answer the questions: http://naomi8busins3.weebly.com/promoting.html and www.nandos.co.uk

## 1.1.3 Working conditions in the hospitality and catering industry

## Employment contracts and working hours

A **contract** is a formal document that is designed to protect both the employee and the employer. It will explain the duties and responsibilities of the role, rules and procedures, as well as details of working days and hours, pay, holiday entitlement, sickness pay, notice and pension arrangements.

Table 1.8 presents details of the different types of employment contract.

**Table 1.8 Types of employment contract**

| Type of contract | How it works |
|---|---|
| Casual | Usually issued for those covering for a sick colleague or working at times where there is more demand. Casual workers are entitled to sickness pay and holiday pay based on hours worked. |
| Full-time (permanent or temporary) | Working days and hours are specified; workers are entitled to sickness and holiday pay. If you are employed on a full-time temporary basis then your contract would be for a fixed time (for example, six months). |
| Part-time (permanent or temporary) | As above, but with reduced sickness and holiday pay because this is calculated **pro rata** (that is, depending on how many hours are worked). |
| Seasonal | Seasonal work is temporary work that usually occurs during a business' busiest times. In hospitality and catering, this is likely to be during holiday periods. |
| Zero-hours contract | A contract between an employer and a worker in which no minimum hours are stated and the worker does not have to accept the work when it is offered; workers are entitled to the National Minimum Wage (if aged under 23) or National Living Wage (aged 23 and over) and holiday pay. The contract can be terminated at any time with no notice. |

### Key terms

**Contract** a formal document designed to protect both employee and employer

**Pro rata** proportional/proportionally; how much you are paid depends on how many hours you work

**Split shift** a shift that is split into two parts, for example lunchtime and evening

## Working hours

The Working Time Regulations state that you cannot work longer than 48 hours a week, calculated as an average over 17 weeks. If you are under 18, you can't work more than 8 hours a day or more than 40 hours a week. Many people in the hospitality and catering industry have to work long and unsociable hours, including late nights and weekends. Chefs may also have to do **split shifts**, where they work lunchtimes and evenings.

### Activity

Explain the advantages and disadvantages of each of the different types of contract.

# Remuneration and benefits

Remuneration is the money you are paid for working.

## A salary

A **salary** is the payment made by an employer to an employee. The details of the salary will be set out in the employee's employment contract. The salary will usually be a fixed amount for a certain period of time, for example they may receive a weekly, monthly or annual salary.

## A wage (hourly)

A **wage** is money paid by an employer to an employee in exchange for work done. It is done on an hourly rate that is multiplied by the number of hours worked.

## Holiday entitlement

Most workers are legally entitled to 28 days (5.6 weeks) of paid holiday a year. An employer can include bank holidays in this allowance. Full-time workers who work a five-day week must receive at least 28 days' paid annual leave a year. Part-time workers are entitled to a reduced amount of paid holiday depending on the number of days/hours they work. For example, if they work three days a week, they must get at least 16.8 days' leave a year ($3 \times 5.6$).

## Pension

A pension is an investment fund that an employee and their employer pay in to, which is paid out when the employee retires from work.

## Sickness pay

Sickness pay protects employees in that they will still get paid if they are too ill to work. An employee's sickness pay entitlement will be included in their contract, which will state how much they will be paid and for how long. The government sets the rate of Statutory Sick Pay (SSP) and an employer cannot pay less than this.

## Rates of pay

Employees are paid a certain amount per hour, week or month, at a rate agreed with an employer. The level of pay will depend on an employee's age, experience, their role and the level of responsibility involved in their job.

The National Minimum Wage is the minimum pay per hour to which workers above school-leaving age are entitled. Staff aged 23 and above should get the National Living Wage, which is higher than the National Minimum Wage. Apprentices are entitled to an apprentice rate if they are under 19, or aged 19 and over in the first year of their apprenticeship. In 2022, the apprentice rate was £4.81 an hour.

Once someone is 19 or older, and in the second year of their apprenticeship, pay switches to the National Minimum Wage. For many apprentices, this can mean a significant pay rise after completing the first year of their scheme/course.

These rates change every year, on 1 April.

---

**Key terms**

**Salary** a fixed payment from an employer to an employee per set period, for example monthly or annually

**Wage** money paid by an employer to an employee in exchange for work done; usually an hourly rate

---

# Tips, bonuses and rewards

Workers in hotels and the hospitality sector can benefit from other remuneration on top of their salaries. This can include tips, service charges, subsidised food and accommodation, and bonuses.

In the UK, restaurant tips are generally between 10 and 20 per cent of the bill, but can be higher when excellent service is provided. Tips are usually divided between the staff.

▲ **Leaving a tip**

If you pay a service charge when you stay at a hotel, eat at a restaurant or go on a cruise, this will be distributed among the staff members for providing service to customers.

Bonuses are generally linked to performance. Employers may pay a bonus to workers based on the good financial results of a team and/or individual.

## Activity

Explain the remuneration and benefits of working in the hospitality and catering industry.

# The fluctuating needs of the industry

## Supply and demand for staffing at peak times, large events, seasonally and according to location

The hospitality industry is the third-largest employer in the UK, contributing 3.2 million jobs through direct employment in the industry and a further 2.8 million indirectly. The hospitality and catering industry normally accounts for more part-time than full-time contracted positions.

Factors that affect demand are whether it is a weekday or the weekend, time of year, economic conditions and situations such as the impact of the Covid-19 pandemic, which forced businesses to close and/or diversify in order to be Covid-safe and adhere to government requirements. (See page 34 for more information on the economy.)

There is greater demand for staff at seasonal times, such as summer and bank holidays, when large events take place (such as festivals), especially in tourist destinations. The UK's departure from the European Union (EU) may have had an impact on the availability of staff.

## Knowledge check

1 Explain how a contract protects an employee.
2 State one advantage and one disadvantage of a zero-hours contract.
3 What is a split shift?
4 Identify one benefit you may receive if you work in a hotel.
5 When might there be increased demand for staff in a restaurant in a tourist destination?

### Activity

Visit the website www.indeed.com to carry out some research on seasonal work and then answer the following questions.

1 What is seasonal work?
2 How does it work?
3 What types of seasonal work are available and how would you get a seasonal job?

### Extension activity

Imagine you are applying for a seasonal job in a restaurant. Write a paragraph on why you would be suitable. (You can refer to the personal attributes in Table 1.5 on page 25.)

### Case study

Costa Coffee is one of the UK'S fastest-growing coffee shop chains. Like other businesses within the hospitality and catering industry, it has faced many challenges and has had to continually adapt and change.

Costa has recognised some key features of the takeaway coffee market:
- The importance of customer self-service
- The increased use of technology
- The need to protect the environment.

They have responded by investing £20 million in drive thrus and new store openings. They have developed Costa Express self-service machines and are committed to sustainability by promoting reusable cups and recycling and sourcing their coffee beans responsibly. Coffee can also be delivered direct to you at work or at home via three different apps, and they also offer a click and collect service.

### Question

Describe the changes Costa coffee has made to respond to changes in the market.

### Further reading

https://www.costa.co.uk/business/costa-express

https://www.thegrocer.co.uk/finance/costa-coffee-invests-20m-in-drive-thrus-and-new-store-openings/670148.article

https://mtpak.coffee/2022/05/exploring-the-unstoppable-rise-of-costa-coffee-brand/

## 1.1.4 Contributing factors to the success of hospitality and catering provision

## Basic costs

There are three different types of costs that have an impact on the success of a hospitality and catering business:

1 labour costs, which are the salaries and wages for all staff connected to the business
2 material costs, which are the costs of things such as ingredients and consumables, for example napkins and cleaning materials
3 overheads, which are costs such as rent, energy, water, telephone, internet, Wi-Fi, insurance, furniture and furnishings.

Costs can also be split into:

- **variable costs** – costs that can change depending on the amount of business the establishment does, such as the cost of food and drink
- **fixed costs** – costs that are always the same, such as rent, insurance and energy (these may increase or decrease at some point in time, however, depending on the business).

## Calculating gross profit and net profit

A business needs to be able to calculate how much profit it makes. There are two types of profit that a business will need to know:

1 **gross profit** is the money that is left over when food costs have been deducted from sales income
2 **net profit** is the money left over when all costs (material, labour and overheads) have been deducted from sales income.

## Example

A restaurant business took £200,000 in food and drink sales over a year. Its total food costs were £55,000, labour costs were £53,500 and overheads were £39,100.

Gross profit would be:

£200,000 − £55,000 = £145,000

Net profit would be:

£200,000 − (£55,000 + £53,500 + £39,100) = £200,000 − £147,600 = £52,400

### Key terms

**Variable costs** costs that change (vary) depending on the amount of business an establishment does, for example amount of stock purchased

**Fixed costs** costs that are constant (for example rent and energy bills) as opposed to other, fluctuating business expenses

**Gross profit** the amount of money remaining when the cost of goods sold (food and drink in this case) has been deducted

**Net profit** the money remaining when all costs (material, labour and overheads) have been deducted from sales income

# How the economy can impact business

The state of the economy can have an impact on business in the following ways.

## Strength of the economy

When the economy is strong, customers have more money to spend on leisure activities and eating out; when the economy is weak, customers may not have as much disposable income to spend.

## Value added tax (VAT)

**VAT** is a tax that has to be added on to a sale, raising money for the government from consumer spending. The standard rate of VAT as of June 2022 is 20 per cent. Some foods are exempt from VAT, but it must be added to services.

VAT is calculated quarterly (every three months) by completing a VAT return and submitting it to HM Revenue & Customs (HMRC). The VAT return records:

- total sales and purchases
- how much VAT is owed
- how much can be reclaimed.

VAT needs to be budgeted for as it could amount to a large bill that will eat into profit. If the rate of VAT goes up, businesses may need to increase their charges to cover this additional cost.

## The value of the pound and the exchange rate

If the rate of exchange represents good value for consumers in other countries, they may choose to travel to the UK and spend money in the hospitality and catering sector. UK customers may stay in the UK if the exchange rate is poor. The value of the pound can also have an impact on things such as the cost of food.

> **Key term**
>
> **VAT** a tax added to goods and services; the standard rate is currently 20 per cent

> **Activity**
>
> Explain the impact that Covid-19 has had on the hospitality and catering industry. For example, what changes did hospitality and catering businesses make in order to stay in business?
>
> A useful place to start is the website of the Office for National Statistics (www.ons.gov.uk) where you can find details of Covid's impact on the UK hospitality sector from January 2020 to June 2021.

# Environmental needs and impacts within the industry

Being an environmentally friendly business, by promoting sustainability and using as few natural resources as possible, appeals to customers, and more customers should mean more profit. Keeping environmental costs to a minimum can also reduce overall costs, which also increases profit. An example of an environmental cost is the disposal of waste.

Today, there is generally an increased awareness of environmental issues. Customers are interested in food provenance (where food comes from) and in establishments' food waste policies.

## Seasonality

Buying foods when they are in season is a more cost-effective approach as they are in plentiful supply. Buying locally when foods are in season supports local farmers and also reduces the environmental cost of transporting foods over long distances. Customers like to know that restaurants are using ingredients that are in season.

## Sustainability

To sustain our environment, we need to maintain and look after it by:

- using less energy
- reducing the consumption of water
- avoiding waste
- recycling and reusing as much as possible.

### Reduce

#### *Reducing energy and water use*

There are many ways that energy and water can be saved in the hospitality and catering industry; many of them also reduce costs and therefore help to maximise profits.

▲ **Strawberries are an example of a seasonal food**

Methods include:

- installing solar panels
- installing double glazing and insulation to keep heating bills down
- using low-energy light bulbs
- buying energy-efficient appliances
- turning off lights when not in use or having automatic sensors for lights
- using dishwashers and washing machines only for full loads
- installing showers in hotel bedrooms rather than baths
- asking guests to reuse towels.

## Reuse

Food accounts for a large percentage of the total costs in a catering establishment. It is therefore essential to know how much a recipe is going to cost to make and that dishes are costed accurately. Food costs need to be controlled so that the establishment makes a profit and stays in business. Food that is left over can be reused to make another dish. For example:

- leftover potato can be used in a frittata or mashed and used in fishcakes
- stale bread can be used to make breadcrumbs
- leftover croissants or brioche can be made into a bread and butter-style pudding
- leftover cake can be used to make trifles or tiramisu.

### Activity

Find a recipe and a method for each of the following leftover foods:
- mashed potato
- cooked chicken
- six croissants
- quarter of a jar of mayonnaise
- large carrots that need using up.

### Extension activity

Find one sweet and one savoury recipe that uses a food that is sometimes wasted. Foods most commonly wasted are bread, milk, potatoes, cheese and apples.

Other things can be reused too. For example:

- refillable dispensers can be used for toiletries such as shower gel and shampoo in hotel bedrooms
- washable cloths can be used rather than disposable ones
- metal drinking straws can be used instead of plastic or paper ones.

## Recycle

Ways in which the hospitality and catering industry can recycle include:

- recycling as much packaging as possible, such as glass, paper, cardboard, plastics and cans
- having recycling bins in hotels and guest houses.

# New technology

Technology is evolving and changing rapidly, and it is important for businesses to keep up with new developments such as those described below.

# Cashless systems

The vast majority of establishments now accept contactless card payments, cashless payments or payments made via bank card details stored on a smartphone.

▲ **Cashless, contactless payment using a smartphone**

# Innovative digital technology

There are many ways in which digital technology is used in hospitality and catering.

■ Computers and computer systems are needed to run most businesses. All information can be stored and updated electronically. Orders can be taken electronically on tablets and sent direct to the kitchen, or customers can use digital menus to order at their table using a smartphone.

■ Rooms, restaurants and meals can be booked online or via an app.

■ Smartphones can be used as door keys in hotels, via an app on the phone instead of magnetic cards.

■ Interviews or meetings, for example with clients or suppliers, can be held online using software such as Google Hangouts, Microsoft Teams or Zoom.

■ Recruiting and interviewing can be done online, reducing the need to travel to an interview and therefore taking up less time.

# The impact of different types of media

In order to succeed, a hospitality and catering business will use a variety of media to attract new customers and maintain its customer base. Different media are used to promote a business so that customers know it exists, to persuade them to visit and pay for its services, and to convince customers that the business is providing quality products and services. Various media are also used to build a relationship with customers, creating a positive image. The impact of media can be both positive and negative (see Table 1.9).

Table 1.9 **Positive and negative impacts of different types of media**

| Type of media | Positive impacts | Negative impacts |
|---|---|---|
| Printed media (newspapers and magazines) | Newspapers and magazines are visually appealing. People often like to keep magazines at home to reread or share with others. Any advertising or an article about a business can be reread.<br><br>Many people still read print and prefer it to digital.<br><br>It is a good option for local targeting, for example getting an article about a business or an advertisement into a local newspaper. | If your business is global then print media may not reach a global audience; it tends to be more local.<br><br>Planning an effective advertisement or article, and making it ready for print, can be time consuming.<br><br>It can also be expensive, and a small advertisement or article may not be noticed if it is printed alongside many others. |
| Broadcast (television and radio) | Television has a powerful impact as it mixes both sight and sound, and can evoke emotions. A television is present in the vast majority of homes so it reaches a large audience.<br><br>Businesses can use radio as a way of promotion as it can reach local audiences, is not as expensive as television, and the promotion can be played numerous times during the day and night. | It is very expensive to produce an item or an advertisement on television. Some people do not watch live television, but prerecord or watch using online catch-up services, allowing them to skip advertisements.<br><br>Radio advertising relies on getting the attention of a listener; however, people are often doing something else while listening such as driving or DIY, so not paying full attention. |
| Internet (social media and websites) | Online reviews on platforms such as Tripadvisor can market a business effectively when someone leaves a positive review and can allow the customer to make a more informed choice.<br><br>Social media platforms such as Facebook and Twitter allow a business to have a better understanding of its customers and keep in contact with them; a business can also advertise on these sites.<br><br>Customers can upload videos of their visits on video-sharing sites such as YouTube. Hotels and restaurants can also upload promotional videos.<br><br>Websites can provide useful information, such as menus and online booking capabilities.<br><br>Having a social media presence is a cost-effective way of being in touch with large numbers of customers; these networks can also be joined free of charge. | Negative online reviews can be very damaging to a business. Often someone will leave a negative review having not mentioned any problem at the time of their visit and therefore not giving the establishment the opportunity to put things right.<br><br>It can be very time consuming to interact with every comment made on social media.<br><br>Once information has been posted to social media it is effectively permanent – it is extremely difficult to delete, so any negative messages could be shared and reposted to a wide variety of sites.<br><br>If some posts are not thought through, or are badly worded, they can prove embarrassing for a business. |
| Competitive (other establishments) | A business always needs to be aware of its **competition**.<br><br>Monitoring the competition regularly is crucial, for example visiting the competitor as a customer, checking its website, reading comments on sites such as Tripadvisor so you can ensure you are offering competitive prices, deals and discounts.<br><br>Reviewing the competition enables you to evaluate your own business, for example to ensure you are giving value for money and high-quality service. Looking at other competitors allows you to have a competitive advantage – this is a distinguishing feature you have that can give you an advantage over your competitors, for example a star chef; a fast, reliable home-delivery service; an original menu; using high-quality organic ingredients; or offering a wide selection of vegan choices. | A business may feel the need to keep updating its products and services to compete with other businesses.<br><br>If there are competitors in the same areas pricing can become an issue, so a business may have to re-evaluate its unique selling point (USP). |

## Knowledge check

1 State three different costs that have an impact on the success of a hospitality and catering business.

2 Describe the difference between variable and fixed costs.

3 State what is meant by VAT.

4 Explain two reasons why it is advantageous for a catering business to use seasonal food.

5 State two ways in which digital technology could be used in a hotel.

### Activity

An independent coffee shop is opening on the same road as a large coffee shop chain.

Design an article to promote this new business that will be used on its social media platform.

### Key term

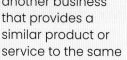

**Competition** another business that provides a similar product or service to the same target customers

### Case study

Eco-friendly hotels are committed to sustaining the environment. An example of an eco-friendly hotel is Dukes Hotel in London. The measures it has put in place include:

- using local and seasonal produce
- a wide-ranging recycling scheme
- using biodegradable cleaning products
- having boilers that are energy efficient
- replacing small plastic bottles with refillable dispenser bottles for toiletries
- all disposable plastic has been replaced with environmentally friendly alternatives.

*Source*: www.countryandtownhouse.co.uk/travel/londons-eco-friendly-hotels/

#### Questions

1 Do some research on what hotels are doing to become more sustainable.

2 Use this information write a report on what hotels can do to become more sustainable.

# Practice questions

1. State **two** reasons why vending machines may be popular in hospitals. (2 marks)

2. State **two** personal attributes you would look for when appointing waiting staff. (2 marks)

3. There is a range of employment opportunities in the hospitality and catering industry. Identify **one** job opportunity in each of the following areas. (2 marks)
   a. The hotel kitchen
   b. Buildings and grounds

4. Kim has her own small business selling sandwiches and hot and cold drinks for take away. Her customers are mainly office staff who work on a nearby business park. Kim wants to ensure her business is environmentally friendly.

   Describe **two** measures she could take that would help sustain the environment. (4 marks)

5. Many people use social media on a daily basis. Describe the positive impact on a business of using social media. (8 marks)

# 1.2 How hospitality and catering providers operate

**What will I learn?**

In this topic you will gain knowledge and understanding of the following areas:

1.2.1 The operation of the front and back of house

1.2.2 Customer requirements in hospitality and catering

1.2.3 Hospitality and catering provision to meet specific requirements

**Getting started**

1 How would you plan out a catering kitchen? Think about what equipment you would need and where you would put it.

2 How could you make sure your kitchen is going to operate hygienically and efficiently?

## 1.2.1 The operation of the front and back of house

### Workflow of the front of house

The front of house covers the following areas:

- reception/counter service
- bar with seating area
- lounge with seating area
- dining area
- toilets and cloakroom.

Restaurants and hotels can be busy, with customers moving around between different areas. There should be a logical layout so that people can move easily from one area to another. Reception should be clearly signposted and ideally lead on to the bar, lounge, dining areas and toilets. Larger establishments may have a dedicated floor for reception and another for dining.

The **workflow** of the front of house describes the flow of food and drinks from the catering kitchen and bar to customers in the dining areas, bars or lounges.

The front of house needs to be designed for the following operational activities:

- reception – where customers check in and out, book tables and find out what facilities are offered both in the establishment and in the local area
- lounge – this is usually a social area with seating where guests can relax with a drink or wait for their table
- bar – an area where drinks can be ordered, which usually has bar stools, tables and chairs
- restaurant/dining area – an area where guests can sit and eat a meal
- toilets and cloakroom – where guests can leave their coats and use the facilities.

▲ **Checking in at reception**

**Key term**

**Workflow** in the front of house, the flow of food and drinks from the catering kitchen and bar to customers in the dining areas, bars or lounges

41

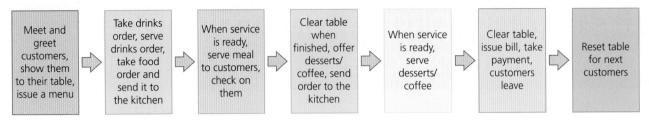

▲ **An efficient workflow pattern for the front of house**

## Workflow of the catering kitchen

The layout of a catering kitchen needs to be planned carefully to make sure that it is hygienic and enables staff to work efficiently. It is important that the workflow is in one direction – the backtracking and crossover of materials and products must be avoided in order to prevent cross-contamination.

The catering kitchen needs to be designed for the following operational activities:
- the receiving and storage of goods
- preparation of food for cooking
- cooking food
- dishing up food and presenting it for service
- service – serving the food to customers
- cleaning and maintaining the kitchen area.

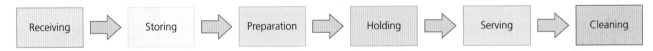

▲ **An example of a workflow**

The layout will vary depending on the size of the kitchen and the types of food it produces. The kitchen should be organised into separate areas to allow efficient workflow and to prevent food becoming contaminated. When food is delivered to the kitchen, it will need to be stored, prepared and finally served to customers. It is most logical if the layout of the kitchen allows for each of these stages in order. This means that when food is delivered it is separated and then stored according to the type of food and storage temperature required. For example, raw meat may be stored covered in a fridge on the bottom shelf away from cooked foods. After this, the raw meat will be prepared in a separate area away from cooked foods. Once cooked, it will be served to customers in the service area.

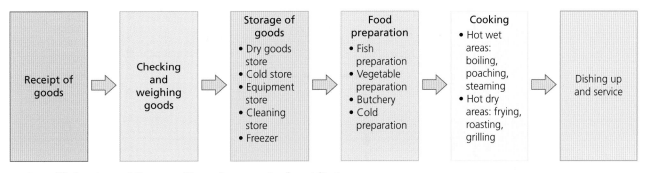

| Receipt of goods | | Checking and weighing goods | | Storage of goods<br>• Dry goods store<br>• Cold store<br>• Equipment store<br>• Cleaning store<br>• Freezer | | Food preparation<br>• Fish preparation<br>• Vegetable preparation<br>• Butchery<br>• Cold preparation | | Cooking<br>• Hot wet areas: boiling, poaching, steaming<br>• Hot dry areas: frying, roasting, grilling | | Dishing up and service |

▲ **An efficient workflow pattern for a catering kitchen**

The aim of a good kitchen workflow is to prevent cross-contamination and reduce the risk of food poisoning.

- The fridges, freezers and ambient food storage areas (where items such as cans, unopened jars, flour, sugar and other items that do not need to be stored in the fridge or freezer are kept) should be near the delivery areas.
- Vegetables should be stored and then prepared in the same area to prevent soil spreading to other foods.
- Raw meat and poultry should be kept separate from other foods.
- Waste food and other rubbish should be covered and kept by the outside door.

See page 75 for more information on food safety.

▲ **A commercial kitchen**

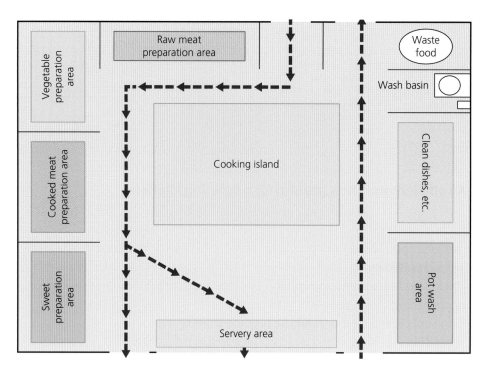

▲ **Kitchen design demonstrating good workflow**

# Equipment and materials

Kitchen equipment is very important to the success of the business and it is expensive to buy, so care must be taken in the use and management of each piece.

## Large equipment

### Large conventional oven

Ovens work using either gas or electricity and are used for baking and roasting. Convection ovens have a fan that circulates the air to create an even temperature so that large quantities of the same food can be cooked quickly and evenly. It is important that ovens are cleaned regularly and maintained to ensure temperature and time control are accurate.

### Glass chiller

A glass chiller is where glasses can be stored. When stored in a glass chiller, glasses stay cold and are given a frosted appearance that is attractive to customers and keeps drinks cool in hot temperatures. Glass chillers will also sanitise glasses in a very short period of time.

### Floor-standing food mixer

▲ **Floor-standing mixer**

Floor-standing mixers are used to mix large quantities of dough, batter or cake mixes quickly. Their capacity can vary from 10 to 40 litres. They have extremely powerful motors to mix and whisk large quantities. Many have different attachments that can be used depending on what is being made, such as a whisk for meringues and a dough hook for bread. They are extremely heavy pieces of equipment, which is why they are positioned on the floor. They need to be cleaned regularly.

## Deep fat fryers

Deep fat fryers are thermostatically controlled containers that are filled with oil and heated via an electric element. They offer a much safer way of deep frying than using a pan, as the frying is done in a sealed container and the temperature controlled so there is less risk of the fryer overheating. Deep fat fryers are used to deep-fry foods such as chips, fish, churros and doughnuts. The oil should be changed regularly, particularly if strongly flavoured foods such as onion bhajis are cooked in the fryer.

## Hot water urns

Commercial water boilers (urns) are used to boil large quantities of water, so are extremely useful to businesses like mobile catering kitchens. They are filled with water, a lid placed on them and then the urn is switched on. Once the water comes to the boil, a thermostat within the urn will keep the water at a constant temperature. Urns can be electric or gas powered. Care should be taken to make sure they do not boil dry if all the water is used, and they should be switched off when not in use.

## Walk-in fridge-freezer

A walk-in fridge-freezer can be fitted with shelving to make **stock rotation** easier. (Stock rotation is when the items that need to be used first are at the front of a shelf.) This also allows large quantities of foods to be kept chilled or frozen at any one time. Walk-in fridge-freezers keep high-risk foods such as meat and dairy products chilled at between 1°C and below 5°C, and frozen foods at −18°C or below.

## Standing bain-marie

A standing bain-marie keeps cooked food warm and ready to eat. It is a gentle way of keeping food warm, so the food does not dry out. In a wet-heat bain-marie, a food pan is placed in hot water, which is gently heated to a set temperature. A dry bain-marie is where a food pan is heated directly so the hot water is not needed.

A standing bain-marie is mounted on the floor. One advantage of this is that it can be placed close to where the food is being served.

**Key term**

**Stock rotation** the practice of using the product with the shortest shelf life before using a similar one with a longer shelf life

▲ **A bain-marie is often used in places such as cafeterias**

## Steamer

When food is steamed it cooks gently with very little water, so foods such as vegetables and fish keep their colour and texture. It is also a healthy way of cooking because it retains the food's vitamins and minerals and does not use fats or oils. A steam oven is designed to cook large quantities of food, such as vegetables, on shelves. There are also smaller steamers available, such as electric steamers and steamers designed for cooking on a hob.

## Pass-through dishwasher and glass washer

Commercial dishwashers are a crucial piece of equipment in busy kitchens as they save time on washing up. A pass-through dishwasher and glass washer is perfect for a large commercial kitchen as it saves time and is far more efficient than washing up by hand. It works by having one side of the machine loaded with dirty plates and glasses, which then pass through the cleaning cycles and come out clean on the other side of the machine. Some will wash up to 80 racks of dishes in an hour. These dishwashers need to be managed to ensure that they are loaded and emptied as soon as required.

## Hotplates

The hotplate is often referred to as the pass. It is where the service staff come to collect prepared food from the kitchen to take to the customer. The hotplate should have all the items needed for the food to be served, such as plates and dishes. The food to be taken to the customer is usually placed on the hotplate, where it will warm through and keep warm.

▲ **Example of a hotplate area**

Hotplates run on either gas or electricity and should be switched on in advance of service to ensure they are hot enough. Both kitchen and waiting staff need to manage their time and communication to ensure that food is served quickly and efficiently, to avoid the food drying out or becoming a food safety risk.

## Activity

Find a picture of each of the following large pieces of equipment and label them:

- large convection oven
- glass chiller
- floor-standing food mixer
- deep fat fryer
- hot water urn
- walk-in fridge-freezer
- standing bain-marie
- steamer
- pass-through dishwasher and glass washer
- hotplate.

### Extension activity

Annotate each picture with details of the cost of the equipment and its main use.

## Materials for cleaning

Materials for cleaning that are used frequently in a catering kitchen include:

- detergents – to remove dirt and grease
- disinfectants – to destroy bacteria
- sanitisers – usually in the form of a spray for cleaning and disinfecting
- antibacterial hand wash and hand gel
- paper towels if hand driers are not used
- kitchen cloths – disposable cloths, which can be thrown away after use, or non-disposable cloths, which can be washed and reused
- bin liners – to be used and disposed of at the end of the day; bins need to be cleaned thoroughly as part of a cleaning schedule.

## First aid kit

A first aid kit should contain the items necessary to deal with the minor injuries that can occur in a catering kitchen. The most common of these are cuts and burns. A first aid kit will usually contain items such as plasters, dressings, bandages, eye wash and antiseptic wipes.

## Safety materials

The safety materials used in a catering kitchen are:

- aprons
- tabards
- disposable gloves
- face masks
- oven gloves
- cling film, foil and parchment paper for wrapping and storing food.

## Small equipment

A catering kitchen uses a range of items of small equipment. Table 1.10 describes how they are used.

Table 1.10 **Small equipment used in a catering kitchen**

| Small equipment | Use |
|---|---|
| Food processor | Used to mix, chop, slice and grate |
| Hand-held food mixer | Used to beat and whisk smaller amounts of food quickly, such as batters for cakes and biscuits |
| Liquidiser or blender | Blends solid food into liquid, such as soups and smoothies |
| Mincer | A stand-alone piece of equipment that minces meat into small pieces |
| Table-top mixer | Used to beat and whisk larger quantities of food<br><br>Will often have attachments, such as a dough hook to knead bread or a mincer for meat |

# Utensils

Catering kitchens use a range of utensils. Table 1.11 presents details of the most common utensils used.

Table 1.11 **Utensils used in a kitchen**

| Name of utensil | Use |
|---|---|
| Baking sheet/tins | Cooking food in an oven |
| Balloon whisk | Whisking, adding air to a mixture |
| Colander | Draining liquid |
| Colour-coded chopping boards | Chopping and cutting food; different foods are cut on boards of different colours |
| Fork | Mashing, eating |
| Frying pan | Frying food |
| Measuring jug | Measuring liquid |
| Mixing bowl | Mixing food |
| Palette knife | Lifting food off a baking sheet |
| Pastry brush | Glazing - for example, glazing a pastry pie with egg (see page 185 for more information on glazing) |
| Peeler | Peeling the skin from fruit or vegetables |
| Rolling pin | Rolling out pastry or dough |
| Saucepan | Boiling or simmering foods |
| Sieve | Adding air into mixtures, removing lumps |
| Spatula | Mixing and folding |
| Tablespoon | Measuring 15 ml, folding flour into a whisked mixture (see page 163 for more information on folding) |
| Teaspoon | Measuring 5 ml, stirring tea and coffee |
| Wok | Stir-frying food |
| Wooden spoon | Mixing ingredients together, stirring food on the hob |

# Documentation and administration requirements in a catering kitchen

## Stock controlling systems

All materials, ingredients and equipment used in a catering kitchen are referred to as **stock**.

Correct storage is important to ensure that ingredients remain in the best condition and are therefore safe to eat. Bin cards are labels that are attached to stock items such as flour and sugar, and should show how much there is and how much has been used so the item can be reordered when running low.

A first in, first out (**FIFO**) policy should always be used, to ensure that older stock is used up first before any new stock is ordered.

## Ordering

Today, order sheets are likely to be managed electronically and will include a list of all stock; orders are completed and sent to a supplier when goods are needed.

## Delivery notes

All deliveries of food should be checked and moved to the most appropriate area within 15 minutes of delivery. Dates on packaging need to be checked when deliveries are placed into stores. All goods need to be checked carefully for quality and quantity. Any damaged items should not be accepted and should be returned. Receipts and delivery notes must be kept for records.

## Invoices

**Invoices** are bills sent to someone for goods or services given. An invoice will include information on the cost of the goods supplied or services carried out. Invoices should be sent out regularly, and should contain information such as name and address, date the goods were supplied and the cost. There is usually a date by which payment should be received.

## Food safety documentation

This is information such as temperature charts for checking and recording the temperature of fridges. There will also be evidence of the business adhering to food hygiene and safety regulations, and evidence of food safety training.

**Key terms**

**Stock** all materials, ingredients and equipment used

**FIFO** first in, first out policy used to ensure that older stock is used up first

**Invoice** bill sent to someone for goods or services they have received

## Health and safety documentation

There should be evidence of health and safety certificates for all staff and records of any training undertaken, for example working at height. All businesses must have an accident book in which to report any accidents at work; this may be in electronic format.

# Typical dress code requirements

A **dress code** gives employees in a hospitality and catering business information about the type of clothing they should wear for work.

### Back of house

A chef should look clean and professional. The protective clothing worn must be clean, hygienic and in a good state of repair. This is important to prevent the transfer of bacteria from dirty clothing to food. The uniform should not be worn outside the catering premises as bacteria from elsewhere can be carried into the kitchen.

A chef should wear:

■ a jacket with long sleeves, usually double-breasted, made from cotton to enable them to stay cool while still offering protection from heat, burns and scalds
■ trousers, which should be loose fitting for comfort and made from cotton to enable them to keep cool; loose-fitting trousers can be removed easily if hot liquids are spilled on them
■ an apron – this is worn around the waist, over the trousers, as added protection
■ a hat – called a **toque**, which is worn to prevent hair from falling into food
■ a necktie – neckties used to be worn to prevent sweat from dripping into food; they are not worn as often now due to improved ventilation in kitchens.

Long hair is tied back
Hat or hairnet
Clean teeth
Clean-shaven
Chef's jacket, preferably with long sleeves
Blue plaster used to cover any cuts
Clean hands and nails
Apron from waist to knee
Baggy chef's trousers
Safety shoes with steel toe caps

▲ **Chefs' clothing**

**Activity**

Find a picture of a chef in their uniform. Stick it into your folder or exercise book and annotate each item of clothing with its name.

**Extension activity**

Explain why each item of clothing is worn.

### Front of house

Front-of-house staff have to look smart and clean, to present a positive image. They often have a corporate uniform. A corporate uniform is where people in the same role wear the same clothing; the uniform often includes a company logo.

## 1.2 How hospitality and catering providers operate

Room attendants/chambermaids always have a uniform covered by an apron for cleaning duties. Waiting staff and bar staff have a specific dress code, designed to look smart as well as being hygienic and safe. This will usually include:

- a black skirt/trousers and white shirt/blouse
- long sleeves to cover arms in case of spillages and burns
- low-heeled black shoes for comfort
- keeping long hair tied back
- apron on top of uniform to protect from hot food/drink and spillages
- cloth tucked in waistband for use when carrying hot plates and dishes.

▲ **Dress code for waiting staff**

**Activity**

Find a picture of a member of waiting staff in their uniform. Stick it into your folder or exercise book and annotate each item of clothing with its name and details of why it is worn.

## Knowledge check

1 Explain why it is important to have an efficient workflow in a catering kitchen.
2 State three reasons why a glass chiller is a useful piece of equipment in a bar.
3 State why it is safer to use an electric deep fat fryer than heating a pan of oil.
4 Explain why a FIFO policy is the best way to manage stock.
5 Identify three features of a chef's jacket.

## Activity

Plan a kitchen workflow to show hygienic and efficient practice. The kitchen prepares only sandwiches using cooked meats, cooked fish and cooked eggs, as well as salad vegetables.

## Case study

Alliance is a company that sells uniforms for those working in hospitality and catering. It has recognised that uniforms should be hygienic and comfortable, and should demonstrate professionalism. A new trend is that employers are looking to merge the styles of casual and smart, mainly in dark colours.

### Questions

1   Visit Alliance Online (www.allianceonline.co.uk) and choose and cost a uniform for a chef and for waiting staff.
2   Give reasons for your choice of clothing.

## 1.2.2 Customer requirements in hospitality and catering

## Customer needs

All customers have different needs. Hospitality and catering establishments should aim to ensure that specific customer needs are met.

▲ **A budget hotel will have limited amenities**

## Catering

Different customers may have different requirements for food and drink (see Table 1.12).

**Table 1.12 Possible customer needs in catering**

| Type of customer | Possible customer needs |
| --- | --- |
| Budget travellers | May not require any food or drink due to budgeting and will source their own. May require some out-of-hours basic facilities if arriving late or leaving early to travel. |
| Business people | High level of food and beverage facilities, particularly if holding meetings. They may want a fine dining option. They are unlikely to need self-catering accommodation because they are travelling for work rather than leisure. |
| Families | May require a fast-food option or a restaurant with a children's menu. Self-catering in a property may allow a family more flexibility. |
| Tourists travelling for leisure | May require only a fridge if they are out and about exploring and want to have some element of self-catering. An option to eat in is needed. |

## Equipment

Different customers may have different requirements for equipment.

**Table 1.13 Possible customer equipment needs**

| Type of customer | Possible customer needs |
|---|---|
| Budget travellers | Very few needs as wanting to pay as little as possible, so may just require a room and bed, with Wi-Fi to plan trips. |
| Business people | Fast Wi-Fi to be able to work efficiently while away from the office. |
| Families | Wi-Fi, especially if the children are playing online games. Beds that fold away to leave more space when not sleeping, TV or gaming facilities. |
| Tourists travelling for leisure | Wi-Fi to plan sightseeing trips, coffee- and tea-making facilities in room, maps and magazines relating to the local area. |

## Accommodation

Different customers may have different requirements for accommodation.

▲ **A youth hostel is suitable for those on a limited budget**

**Table 1.14 Possible customer needs for accommodation**

| Type of customer | Possible customer needs |
|---|---|
| Budget travellers | May be happy to share facilities and a room. They need only a basic room to sleep in, to keep costs down. |
| Business people | An executive room, which will usually be large and have a desk for them to be able to work from. |
| Families | A large room with enough sleeping space for everyone, or rooms with connecting doors. They may prefer a property with a kitchen, lounge and bedrooms, which will allow them more flexibility, particularly in poor weather. |
| Tourists travelling for leisure | A room with comfortable seating, a fridge or minibar. They may wish to be in one area, so may prefer a property with a kitchen, lounge and bedrooms. |

**Activity**

Look at the website for a hotel chain such as Premier Inn or Travelodge. What accommodation, catering and equipment does it have that would suit someone on a budget?

# Customer rights and inclusion

Everyone should be treated fairly, regardless of age, sex, race, sexual orientation, disability, religion or gender. For example:

- a business cannot discriminate against mothers who are breastfeeding
- when providing facilities or services, it is unlawful to discriminate against a transgender person
- a business must not discriminate against a carer because they are caring for someone with a disability.

▲ **Access signage for people with disabilities**

Businesses need to make reasonable adjustments to help individuals with disabilities access their facilities and services. For example, where possible adjustments should be made to stairways, steps, parking areas, entrances, exits, doors and gates, toilets and washing facilities, and lifts and escalators.

Businesses must not allow their customers to be subjected to harassment that could disturb a person's dignity or create an intimidating or hostile environment for them.

Customers are also protected by a number of acts of legislation.

## The Consumer Protection Act 1987

This gives consumers the right to claim compensation against the producer of a defective product if it has caused damage, death or personal injury. Manufacturers are legally obliged to put certain information on products, such as health and safety messages on equipment, that may be used by customers when eating out or staying in accommodation.

## The Consumer Rights Act 2015

This states that all products must be:

- of satisfactory quality – goods shouldn't be faulty or damaged when the consumer receives them
- fit for purpose – goods should be suitable for the purpose for which they are supplied
- as described – the goods supplied must match any description given to the consumer.

This legislation should ensure that a meal ordered matches the description given or that a room booked is fit for purpose, for example hot water is available in the bathroom.

## The UK General Data Protection Regulation (GDPR)

When you buy goods and services, stay at a hotel or sometimes even just visit a website, the organisations you deal with may collect information and data about you, such as your name, address and date of birth. Under GDPR rules, businesses must have a customer's consent to store this information, use it for marketing purposes or share it with other businesses.

## Equality

A business should promote **equality**, treating everyone who accesses its facilities or services fairly, regardless of age, gender, race, sexual orientation, disability, gender reassignment, religion or belief, and must not make assumptions about customers.

## The Equality Act 2010

This protects customers from direct **discrimination** on the basis of:

- age
- disability
- gender reassignment
- pregnancy, maternity and breastfeeding
- race – including ethnicity or national origins, skin colour and nationality
- religion or belief
- marriage or civil partnership
- sex and sexual orientation.

### Key terms

**Equality** being equal, especially in terms of status, rights or opportunities

**Discrimination** the unjust treatment of people, for example on the grounds of race, age or sex

## Knowledge check

1 Identify two catering needs that a family may have when staying at a hotel.
2 Describe the kind of room that would be suitable for a business traveller.
3 State three adjustments a restaurant can make to make it more accessible to someone in a wheelchair.
4 Which act ensures that the goods supplied match the description given to a consumer?
5 Explain how the UK General Data Protection Regulation (GDPR) protects you as a consumer.

### Activity

List the customer needs for catering, accommodation and equipment for a family consisting of two parents and their seven-year-old son, who want to visit a seaside town in the south of England.

#### Extension activity

Look on the internet and choose three places to stay that meet the family's needs, explaining why each place does so.

### Case study

Stradey Park Hotel in Wales is one of many hotels that offer a range of facilities for people with disabilities. It offers specially adapted rooms that have wheel-in showers and shower chairs, as well as:

- wheelchair access
- a level, flat drive
- visual aids such as a large-print menu
- wheelchair ramps
- grab rails.

#### Question

Visit a website such as www.disabledholidays.com and make a list of the wide range of facilities hotels can offer to support customers with disabilities.

## 1.2.3 Hospitality and catering provision to meet specific requirements

Hospitality and catering provision has to adapt to meet the needs of an ever-changing customer climate.

A hospitality and catering business cannot operate without customers, so meeting customers' specific requirements is of the utmost importance.

## Customer requirements/needs

### Lifestyle

**Lifestyle** means how someone chooses to live and what they like to do. Businesses need to take the lifestyles of different groups of people into account – for instance, their disposable income, if they travel and eat out, or stay overnight as part of their work.

### Nutritional needs

The nutritional needs of a customer should be considered carefully when planning a menu. A chef should take into consideration that everyone needs:

- protein for growth, repair and general maintenance of the body
- carbohydrates – the main energy source for the body
- fats – an important source of energy and insulation for the body
- vitamins – responsible for controlling many chemical reactions in the body
- minerals – control many chemical processes and maintain fluid balances in the body
- fibre to help the body get rid of waste (faeces).

More information on this topic can be found in section 2.1, which discusses the importance of nutrition.

**Activity**

Find three different recipes for dishes that match the following brief:
- high in fibre
- low fat
- a good source of starchy carbohydrate.

**Extension activity**

Explain why each dish you have chosen is:
1 high in fibre
2 low fat
3 a good source of starchy carbohydrate.

### Dietary needs

**Dietary needs** are when a customer has a specific or restricted diet. Customers have a wide range of dietary needs, which hospitality and catering establishments have to take into consideration. Examples include food allergies, such as nut allergies, and food intolerances, such as lactose intolerance or gluten intolerance. For more information on food allergies see page 84.

Some people may be vegetarian or vegan for ethical reasons, while others may not eat certain foods for religious reasons.

---

**Activity**

Have a look at a variety of restaurants in your local area.

Identify the dishes that they include on their menus that are suitable for:
1 a vegan
2 a lacto-vegetarian
3 someone with coeliac disease.

**Extension activity**

Suggest some other suitable dishes they could include for people with these dietary needs.

---

# Time available

Today, more people are working longer hours. This can reduce the time and motivation they have to cook meals so, for convenience, they may choose to eat outside the home, buy takeaway food or have food from restaurants delivered to them.

Time may also be limited when someone eats out – for instance, they may be at work and have only a half-hour meal break.

If there is a short amount of time available to cook, serve and eat the food, then the range of food offered on the menu is usually limited. Fast-food outlets have a smaller menu so they can cook and serve food quickly. If there is more time available, a menu can be wider in range and more complex. It is essential that time is managed appropriately by the chef and their team, to ensure that the waiting time for customers to receive food and between courses is acceptable.

# Customer expectations

## Service

Each customer should receive excellent service every time they visit a hospitality and catering establishment. If customers are happy with the service, they are more likely to return and they may recommend it to others. Well-run hospitality and catering businesses will provide ongoing training for their staff, to ensure they are providing the level of service customers expect. All staff should understand what excellent service is, be smart and welcoming, and ensure all customers are well looked after and happy to return. Everyone should be treated as valued customers, with kindness and respect, regardless of their appearance or background. Poor customer service will mean that customers don't return, which could cause the business to fail.

## Value for money

The price that a customer pays for a meal, service or room should be fair. Note that this does not necessarily mean cheap – a room in a luxury hotel will be expensive, but the extra facilities offered may mean that the price is still fair.

▲ **A welcoming receptionist at a hotel**

## Trends

Customers' requirements continue to change and evolve. Hospitality and catering establishments need to keep up with current trends in order to be competitive.

Current customer trends include:
- continued use and development of technology, for example the use of technology and smartphones to book and order services
- the use of social media for information and communication
- ordering food online for delivery
- increased awareness of environmental issues – customers are interested in food provenance (where food comes from) and in establishments' food waste policies
- increase in the numbers of vegetarians and vegans, and a subsequent increase in the number of restaurants catering for them
- menus offering healthier options, reliable allergy information and a variety of choices for people with food intolerances (for example, gluten and dairy).

## Awareness of competition from other providers

A business always needs to be aware of its competition. 'Competition' means another business that provides a similar product or service to the same target customers. A number of strategies are used to ensure that a business attracts and retains customers ahead of its competitors, including monitoring the competition regularly. It is always a good idea to look for a competitive advantage – this is a distinguishing feature that can give a business an advantage over its competitors, such as a star chef; a fast, reliable home-delivery service; an original menu; using high-quality organic ingredients; or offering a wide selection of vegan choices.

# Media influence/interest

The media influences the hospitality and catering industry. It can be used to promote and advertise a business, and it can also offer a forum for customer reviews. The media offers an effective way of stimulating interest in a business. Table 1.15 shows different ways that media can influence a business.

▲ **Deliveroo is an online food delivery company**

Table 1.15 **Media influences**

| Media influence | How it is of interest |
|---|---|
| Delivery | Sites such as Deliveroo and Just Eat can be used to find a restaurant, order food online and have it delivered; this will increase orders and, therefore, profits. |
| Internet searches/maps | These are used to look up places to eat in the local area. It is important for a business to have an online presence; if it is not on the internet, customers may not be aware of it and will go elsewhere. It is important that details are kept up to date, for example on Google Maps. |
| Social media | Businesses receive feedback from customers on sites such as Tripadvisor. This can influence whether customers will visit a restaurant or hotel. Photos of food can be shared on social media sites such as Instagram; these are interesting for other consumers and can influence whether or not they visit. |
| Websites | Websites are used to promote and advertise a business; many people use the internet when researching where to eat or stay. |

## Environmental concerns

Being an environmentally friendly business that promotes sustainability and uses as few natural resources as possible appeals to customers, and more customers means more profit. Keeping environmental costs, such as those for the removal of waste, to a minimum can also reduce overall costs, which also increases profit. Many businesses are reducing the amount of packaging and plastic they use, making changes such as replacing plastic cutlery with recyclable wooden cutlery, restricting the use of paper napkins, and using metal straws rather than plastic or paper ones (plastic straws are already banned in England).

## Seasonality

Seasonality has an impact on the hospitality and catering industry. During high/peak seasons, such as Christmas or the summer holidays, demand can be much higher, so it is important that businesses plan for this in terms of staffing and ordering food and materials.

The main factors that affect seasonality are:
- school holidays
- the weather
- any festival or event in the area.

# Customer demographics

**Demographics** is information about the population of an area, such as the age, gender and income of the people. This information can help businesses to plan what their target market is going to be.

## Age

Different age groups have different requirements from a hospitality and catering establishment.
- A family with a baby or young children will need facilities such as bottle warmers, high chairs, healthy menu choices for children, and rooms with cots or single beds.
- A family with older children and teenagers will want leisure activities such as table tennis, a swimming pool and Wi-Fi for smartphones, tablets and laptops.
- Young travellers usually only want the basics as they are likely to be on a budget; cost-effective food, room only or a shared room in a hostel, sharing facilities such as kitchens, showers and laundry.
- Older people may want leisure activities such as a spa pool, bowling green or golf course.

## Location

Hospitality and catering establishments offer a wide variety of options for customers with specific needs and which can be adapted for different locations and situations.

A pop-up restaurant is often set up in a convenient location, for example near an event or festival, or may appear in peak season only. A mobile van can provide an excellent service, particularly for those in rural communities where access to takeaway and delivery is limited. Hospitality and catering businesses can also be sited in convenient locations close to visitor attractions, such as theme parks. Budget hotels are designed to be in convenient locations, usually near a motorway or airport. Restaurants are often located alongside them, to cater for the budget traveller.

▲ **A mobile food van**

### Activity

You have purchased a mobile food van that you are going to take to different rural villages every weekday evening.
1 What would you specialise in and why?
2 Explain which dishes you would serve and why you think they would be popular.

## Accessibility

Hospitality and catering establishments should provide for all customers, including customers with disabilities and those with assistance dogs. Such customers may prefer a room on the ground floor so stairs can be avoided, or a room that is accessible via a lift. They may need a larger room that has facilities such as grab rails, wet rooms and light switches at a lower height.

## Money available

The choice of food purchased outside the home is affected by household income. Households with two wage earners may have more **disposable income**, which is the money left over for saving or spending after expenditures have been subtracted from income. The more disposable income someone has, the more likely they are to be able to eat out or go on holiday.

### Key term

**Disposable income** the money left over for saving or spending after expenditures have been subtracted from income

# Access to establishments/provision

Hospitality and catering establishments may need to take steps to ensure that they are accessible to all customers. For example:

- customers with disabilities may need help with carrying drinks or trays if a business is self-service or carvery-style
- customers who use wheelchairs will need extra room to manoeuvre to and from their table; this should be managed by waiting staff
- customers with mobility issues may need accessible lifts or ramps to enable them to access all parts of a building, as well as suitable bathroom facilities
- it is useful if the establishment has toilet facilities on the same floor as the restaurant.

Where possible, adjustments should be made to stairways, steps, parking areas, entrances and exits, doors and gates, to allow easy manoeuvrability.

## Knowledge check

1 State two dietary needs that a chef would take into consideration when planning a menu.
2 Explain why people who work long hours may eat out regularly.
3 State what is meant by a competitive advantage, and one way in which it might be achieved.
4 State two reasons why businesses are becoming more environmentally friendly.
5 Define disposable income.

### Activity

Make a revision mind map of all the ways in which hospitality and catering provision meets the specific requirements of customers.

### Case study

The Old Dough Hook Pizza Co was founded in 2017 and produces authentic wood-fired pizzas from a converted van. The business can bake 90 pizzas per hour. Based in Worcestershire, it specialises in weddings, private parties and a range of other events. It also goes to different venues during the week and serves direct to the public.

**Question**

What are the advantages and disadvantages of this style of catering?

**Further reading**

https://theolddoughhook.co.uk/

# Practice questions

1   Complete the table below by matching the names of the following pieces of equipment to their pictures: steamer, pass, floor-standing mixer, bain-marie. Then add a description of what each piece of equipment is used for. (8 marks)

| | Name of equipment | What the equipment is used for |
|---|---|---|
| | | |
| | | |
| | | |
| | | |

2   List these steps in a kitchen workflow in the correct order: holding, receiving, cleaning, storing, serving, preparation. (6 marks)

3   Describe how a hotel can ensure that it provides excellent service to a customer. (6 marks)

4   List the **four** items a chef would typically wear as part of the dress code for a restaurant. (4 marks)

5   A budget traveller wishes to travel around North Wales. They enjoy the outdoors, walking and climbing. Explain what they may need in terms of accommodation and catering. (6 marks)

# 1.3 Health and safety in hospitality and catering

## What will I learn?
In this topic you will gain knowledge and understanding of the following areas:
1.3.1 Health and safety in hospitality and catering provision
1.3.2 Food safety

> **Getting started**
> Mind map and discuss the key safety areas in the hospitality and catering industry.

## 1.3.1 Health and safety in hospitality and catering provision

It is important that the hospitality and catering work environment is safe at all times. It is everyone's responsibility to make sure they follow health and safety rules at work. This will help to prevent accidents and ensure the business is a safe place to work. Both employers and employees have responsibilities for personal safety in the workplace in relation to the following laws.

## Control of Substances Hazardous to Health (COSHH) Regulations 2002

The Control of Substances Hazardous to Health (COSHH) Regulations cover substances that are **hazardous** to health. For example:

- chemicals, such as cleaning materials
- fumes from machinery and cooking processes
- dusts, for example from icing sugar or flour
- vapours from cleaning chemicals, such as oven cleaner
- gases from cookers.

Any substances hazardous to health must be:

- stored, handled and disposed of according to COSHH Regulations
- identified on the packaging or container
- shown in writing and given a risk rating
- labelled as toxic, harmful, irritant, corrosive, explosive or oxidising.

An employer should ensure that employees' use of and exposure to these substances is kept to a minimum. An employee should ensure that they are trained in the use of these substances. They should take note of the international symbols that are used to identify the different types of substances and how they can cause harm.

**Key term**

**Hazardous** risky or dangerous

▲ **Symbols used to identify different types of substances and how they can harm people**

# Health and Safety at Work Act 1974

Employers are responsible for providing a safe workplace that will not cause illness or harm to their employees. This means that employers should ensure:

- equipment is tested for safety and correctly maintained
- chemicals are stored and used correctly, and staff are trained in how to use them
- **risk assessments** are completed
- a **health and safety policy statement** is given to employees that outlines the ways in which the workplace complies with the law
- safety equipment and clothing are provided
- health and safety training is given and is updated regularly.

If any of these things have not been explained to you, you should ask your employer about them.

Employees should ensure that they:

- work in a safe way so they don't put themselves or others in danger
- co-operate with the health and safety rules set by the business
- wear the safety clothing and equipment provided by the business
- report anything that poses a health and safety risk or something that could be a risk.

If employees do something that endangers or hurts someone at work, their employer can discipline them or fire them. They may also be fined, or even imprisoned.

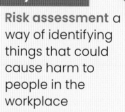

**Key terms**

**Risk assessment** a way of identifying things that could cause harm to people in the workplace

**Health and safety policy statement** a written statement by an employer of its commitment to health and safety for its employees and the public

# Manual Handling Operations Regulations 1992

The Manual Handling Operations Regulations protect employees from injury or accident when they are lifting or moving heavy or awkwardly shaped boxes. The regulations also cover items that are hot, frozen or sharp, which may also need to be carried in the hospitality industry.

Employers must complete a risk assessment whenever items need to be moved, and provide adequate training.

Employees must be trained in correct manual handling techniques and lifting. Equipment for moving items, such as a sack truck or trolley, should be provided when appropriate.

## Lifting

When handling boxes, cartons and trays, there is a correct way to lift:
- always keep your back straight
- bend your knees and use the strength in your arms
- never reach forwards
- keep the item close to your body and make sure you hold the item firmly
- use protective clothing if there are sharp edges on boxes or cartons
- never attempt to carry items that are too heavy – always get help.

▲ **Correct and incorrect lifting techniques**

# Personal Protective Equipment at Work Regulations (PPER) 1992

**Personal protective equipment (PPE)** is clothing or equipment designed to protect the wearer from injury. It is sometimes necessary to wear it when cleaning as the chemicals used in the workplace are often stronger than those normally used at home.

These regulations require employers to provide suitable high-quality protective clothing and equipment to employees who may be exposed to a risk to their health and safety while at work.

PPE can include:

- gloves to protect hands from cleaning materials, and metallic-style gloves to be used when cutting meat
- goggles to prevent eyes being splashed with chemicals
- face masks/face shields to prevent inhalation of any chemical or powder
- long sleeves to prevent contact with skin on arms
- waterproof aprons to be worn on top of clothing.

Signs reminding employees what PPE to wear and when should also be visible. Employees are expected to attend training sessions on how to wear PPE, and to wear it in the workplace as instructed by their employer.

**Key term**

**Personal protective equipment (PPE)** clothing or equipment designed to protect the wearer from injury

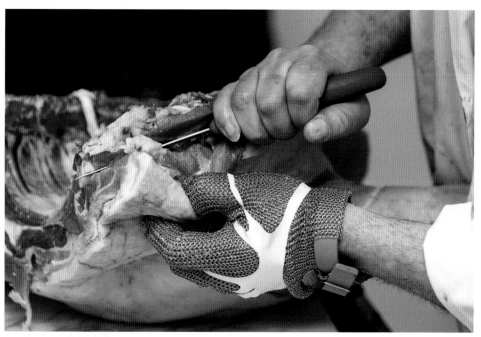

▲ **A butcher could wear reinforced gloves when using sharp knives to cut meat**

# Reporting of Injuries, Diseases and Dangerous Occurrences Regulations (RIDDOR) 2013

 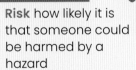
As part of the Health and Safety at Work Act (see above), these regulations require employers to report certain workplace incidents to the **Health and Safety Executive (HSE)**.

An online report form should be submitted directly to the RIDDOR database. These reports cover:

- death and major injuries (for example serious burns)
- dangerous occurrences (for example near-miss events such as the collapse of equipment)
- a case of work-related disease (for example occupational dermatitis, which is a rash you may get if you come into direct contact with certain chemicals)
- flammable gas incidents (for example leaking of gas)
- dangerous gas fittings (for example a faulty gas cooker).

Employers must also keep a record of any injury, disease or dangerous accident, so an employee must ensure that:

- they tell their line manager or union representative if they see any health and safety issue that concerns them
- any injuries at work are recorded in an accident book.

If nothing is done about a health and safety concern that an employee has reported, this inaction can be reported to the HSE.

## Activity

Visit a local hotel, or search the internet for a clip showing you around one.

List all of the safety signs you see, and look for anything that highlights the safety of employees and customers.

### Extension activity

Write a brief report analysing how safe you think the establishment is.

# Risks to health and security

## Risk assessment

A risk assessment should be carried out to identify **risks**. It is a way of identifying things that could cause harm to people in the workplace. All workplaces must have the necessary risk assessments in place.

In a business, there are five steps to risk assessment:

1 Identify the **hazard**.
2 Decide who might be harmed and how.
3 Evaluate the risks and decide on the **controls** (precautions).
4 Record the findings and implement them.
5 Review the assessment and update if necessary.

## Calculating risks when writing a risk assessment

It is possible to calculate whether a level of risk is high, medium or low. To do this, the severity of the hazard and the likelihood of it happening are given a score on a scale of 1 to 5. These figures can then be multiplied together to give a level of risk. The overall aim is to remove or reduce the risk to an acceptable level (as close to 1 as possible).

### Levels of risk

The scales listed in Table 1.16 can be used to calculate level of risk.

**Table 1.16 Scales for level of risk**

| Hazard severity | Likelihood of occurrence | Scale |
|---|---|---|
| Trivial | Remote (almost never) | 1 |
| Minor | Unlikely (occurs rarely) | 2 |
| Moderate | Possible (uncommon) | 3 |
| Serious | Likely (not frequent) | 4 |
| Fatal | Very likely (frequently) | 5 |

**Table 1.17 Levels of risk**

| Low risk 1–8 | Medium risk 9–14 | High risk 15–25 |
|---|---|---|
| Continue but review regularly to ensure controls remain effective | Continue but implement additional controls where possible and monitor regularly | Stop the activity! Identify new controls Activity must not proceed until risks are reduced to a low or medium level |

Level of risk = hazard severity × likelihood of occurrence

As an example, a cut finger using a small knife would be a minor risk (scoring 2 on hazard severity in Table 1.16), which is possible (3 on likelihood of occurence), so the level of risk would be 2 × 3 = 6, making it a low risk on the levels of risk scale in Table 1.17.

## Potential risks to health and security of employees, suppliers and customers

The potential risks identified in Table 1.18 pose a threat to employees, suppliers and customers. Such risks must be controlled by putting measures in place to ensure they are all low or medium risk; no risk should be high.

Table 1.18 **Potential risks to health and security of employees, suppliers and customers**

| Risks to employees | Risks to suppliers | Risks to customers |
|---|---|---|
| Stress | Using equipment | Food poisoning |
| Fatigue | Trip hazards | Food allergies |
| Using equipment | Food and drink spillages | Trip hazards |
| Trip hazards | Inadequate clothing worn | Food and drink spillages |
| Food and drink spillages | Moving and lifting objects | Fire and explosion |
| Using hazardous chemicals | Fire and explosion | Theft |
| Inadequate clothing worn | Injuries | Assault |
| Using electrical appliances | Inadequate lighting | Undesirable people on the premises |
| Moving and lifting objects | Inadequate signage | Terrorist attack |
| Fire and explosion | Fraud | Burglary |
| Bullying and harassment | Theft | Arson |
| Injuries | | |
| Inadequate lighting | | |
| Inadequate ventilation | | |
| Inadequate signage | | |
| Theft | | |
| Assault | | |
| Undesirable people on the premises | | |
| Terrorist attack | | |
| Burglary | | |
| Fraud | | |
| Vandalism | | |
| Arson | | |

## Accident forms

▲ **Example of an accident form**

## 1.3 Health and safety in hospitality and catering

It is important to keep accurate and appropriate records in the catering industry. These may be required during a visit by officials, such as Environmental Health Officers (see page 110), during an inspection, or by the HSE if it is investigating an accident. It is essential to have an accident book with an appropriate accident form that records any details of accidents. An accident record form needs to include the following information:

- details of the accident/injury
- the date, time and location
- how it happened
- what caused it
- what treatment was given
- what steps have been taken to prevent such an accident happening again.

The risk assessment would then need to be reviewed and the accident should be reported to the HSE as stated in the RIDDOR requirements.

As noted above, the Health and Safety at Work Act states that employers are responsible for health and safety training, and for ensuring that this training is updated regularly.

### Activity

A chef working in the kitchen of a bistro has cut their hand while using a blunt knife, which slipped when they were chopping some vegetables. The workplace first aider attempted to stop the bleeding but was unable to do so. The chef had to go to the local minor injuries unit for further treatment.

Complete an accident record form, making sure you include all of the information that is required.

## Knowledge check

1 When handling boxes, cartons and trays there is a correct safe way to lift. Fill in the gaps in the text below using the following words:
back, hold, clothing, knees, arms, help, forwards, heavy
Always keep your _____ straight when lifting. Bend your _____ and use the strength in your _____ . Never reach _____ . Keep the item close to your body and make sure you _____ the item firmly. Use protective _____ if there are sharp edges on boxes or cartons. Never attempt to carry items that are too _____ – always get _____ .

2 List three examples of PPE.

3 List the five steps of writing a risk assessment.

4 Explain what is meant by high risk when completing a risk assessment.

5 Identify three things that should be included on an accident form.

## Activity

Use the internet to find the COSHH symbol for each of the following hazards:
- explosive
- flammable
- oxidising
- corrosive
- harmful
- acute toxicity
- hazardous to the environment
- health hazard
- serious health hazard
- gas under pressure.

## Case study

Health and safety breaches have serious implications. A hotel in London was ordered to pay a £45,000 fine for fire safety failures that placed staff and customers at risk. The owner had to pay the fine or face six months in prison.

During a routine visit by London Fire Brigade, it emerged that:
- there were no smoke detectors
- a fire door was secured open
- the closing mechanism on some fire doors did not work
- rubbish was blocking a first-floor emergency exit; the exit led to a locked gate, which staff could not unlock
- there was no fire risk assessment or evidence of fire safety management
- staff did not know the emergency procedures should a fire occur.

### Questions

1 Visit www.hse.gov.uk/catering and read some of the case studies.
2 Choose one and write up:
   a what happened
   b what should be done to ensure it does not happen again.

## 1.3.2 Food safety

# The HACCP system

**Hazard Analysis and Critical Control Points (HACCP)** is a system that was invented to try to prevent illness caused by eating contaminated foods. It looks carefully at every stage of food production and highlights where contamination could occur, including before and during the production of food. It then puts controls into the system to stop these potential hazards becoming actual hazards, and therefore helps to prevent food poisoning.

The steps of cooking, cooling and storage of food are a priority within the HACCP system as it is during these processes in particular that contamination is more likely to occur.

You will need to know and understand the principles of HACCP for Unit 1. This section on food safety will provide you with the information you need to know about food safety management systems and how these can keep food safe.

## Food safety management systems

It is the law that all food businesses need to have a food safety management system in place. It is the business manager's or owner's responsibility to make sure this food safety management system is kept up to date and followed at all times.

The system identifies the critical points in the process of food production and recognises the hazards that could occur. It considers at what stage something could go wrong, as well as when, where and how it could go wrong. Controls are then put in place to reduce or eliminate the risk. Checks must be in place to make sure this system is applied at all times, to ensure food is safe to eat.

## Risk assessment and record-keeping

Every stage of food production is examined carefully during a risk assessment, to identify what the hazards are and how they could occur. Once they have been identified, controls are put in place to prevent them from becoming actual hazards.

**Hazard analysis** identifies all the stages in the food production process that could cause harm to the consumer – from the beginning, when the ingredients are purchased, transported and delivered, through preparation, cooking and serving, right up to the point when the consumer eats the food.

Records need to be kept (either online or as hard copies) to save this information. When a business is inspected by an **Environmental Health Officer (EHO)**, they will ask to see these records. (More information on EHOs can be found on page 110.)

## Food safety training

All employees who are required to handle food as part of their role must be trained in food safety. They need to know the **critical control points** and how to prevent possible risks from becoming real risks.

The term 'critical control points' refers to all the points where a hazard needs to be removed or controlled.

**Key terms**

**Hazard Analysis and Critical Control Points (HACCP)** a system for identifying and controlling hazards within a food business

**Hazard analysis** analysis that aims to identify the stages in the food production process that could cause harm to the consumer

**Environmental Health Officer (EHO)** council official responsible for inspecting premises involved in food production to ensure that health and safety hazards are minimised

**Critical control points** points in a food production system where hazards need to be removed or reduced to a safe level

# Writing a food safety management plan

The stages of writing a food safety management plan are as follows.

## 1 Identify the hazards

The food we eat must be safe, but it may be contaminated by four types of hazard:

1 physical hazards, for example fragments of glass or plastic from packaging
2 chemical hazards, for example cleaning chemicals
3 biological hazards, for example harmful bacteria
4 food allergens.

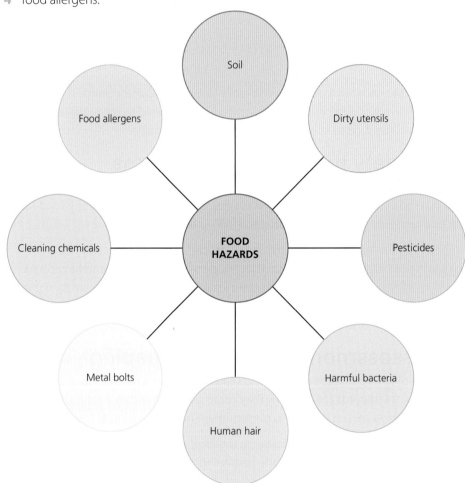

▲ **Hazards in food production**

## 2 Identify the critical control points

Some stages in food production have critical control points. A critical control point is a step in the process at which a control must be applied so that a food safety hazard can be eliminated or reduced to an acceptable standard.

Every critical control point must have an effective control measure. As an example, this could be cooling to prevent the growth of micro-organisms. Micro-organisms are bacteria, yeasts and moulds that can spoil food if they contaminate it and have the correct conditions to grow. Yeasts and moulds can spoil the colour, flavour and texture of food. If certain harmful bacteria (also called pathogenic bacteria) are allowed to grow in food, they can cause food poisoning.

The conditions that bacteria need to grow are:
- moisture
- warmth
- a source of food
- time to grow.

Therefore, cooling food to prevent the growth of micro-organisms takes away one of the conditions – warmth.

It is also important to make sure that the weight of food is within a stated limit, to ensure consistency in cooking. For example, if a supermarket is roasting chickens at a delicatessen counter, the weight of all of the chickens will need to be consistent to make sure that all of them are cooked through at the same time. While they don't need to be *exactly* the same weight, the limits for the weight range need to be written down when the control is decided for the process.

A critical control point could also cover control of time and temperature; for example, food that needs to be chilled should be cooled down within 90 minutes, usually to below 5°C. Critical control points may also be in place to prevent the contamination of foods by allergens, for example the use of separate tongs to serve different foods.

## 3 Set the critical limits

A **critical limit** is the maximum or minimum tolerance to which a physical, chemical or biological hazard or allergen must be controlled at each critical control point. This will prevent, eliminate or reduce a hazard to an acceptable level.

Some critical limits are easy to define, such as the maximum temperature at which a fridge should be working, which ideally is between 0°C and below 5°C. (The legal maximum temperature for a fridge is 8°C.)

## 4 Monitor the critical limits

A **monitoring** system must be set up for each critical control point to ensure the process is under control.

**Key terms**

**Critical limits** upper and lower acceptable limits, for example a fridge temperature should be between 0°C and below 5°C (8°C is the legal maximum)

**Monitoring** observing, watching, checking

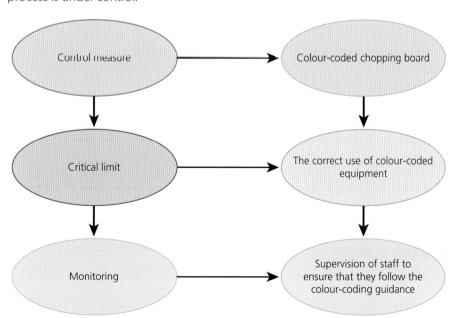

▲ **Critical control points: preventing cross-contamination**

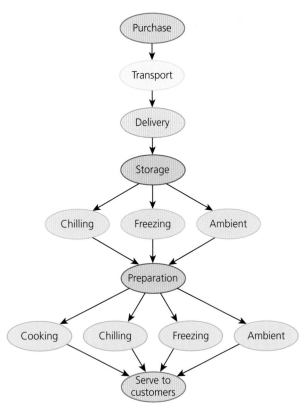

▲ **Example of a HACCP flow chart**

Monitoring of critical control points can be done by a supervisor watching staff to make sure the rules that have been set are being followed.

Colour coding of equipment can help to reduce the likelihood of contamination of food. It classifies food into groups, each of which can be prepared on chopping boards of a particular colour to avoid contamination between different types of foods. Other equipment, such as knives and tongs, are sometimes colour coded too, to reduce contamination. For more on colour coding, see section 1.4.3.

Apart from colour coding, and checks by staff and supervisors, other things that can be monitored are temperatures and timings for cooking, cooling and chilling. There can also be regular observation of equipment and work surfaces to make sure they are clean, or checks of delivery vehicles to make sure they are clean and that foods are delivered at the correct temperature.

## 5 Take corrective action

**Corrective action** is needed when monitoring shows that critical limits haven't been met. This corrective action needs to happen straight away to ensure the safety of food. Some examples of corrective action are:

- if reheated food has not reached 75°C, it should be heated for longer until this temperature has been achieved
- if equipment is not clean after washing up, it should be washed again.

## 6 Have a record system

All food businesses must keep a written (or online) record of their food production process. Information to be recorded includes:

- temperatures of fridges and freezers
- temperatures of foods, taken at various stages of cooking, reheating and serving
- cleaning schedules
- staff training
- delivery records
- names and addresses of suppliers.

This information may be needed in order to prove **due diligence** if a food business is taken to court. Due diligence means that all reasonable care has been taken by a business to prevent harm to food, and food businesses must provide evidence of this (for example that the temperature of fridges has been recorded twice a day).

## 7 Verify the system

This is where the HACCP system is checked to see if it is working. Some aspects may be reviewed, for example how food is cooled and chilled quickly. A process may be repeated and temperatures taken to check whether it is effective. If any processes aren't working well enough, they can be updated to make them better.

---

**Key terms**

**Corrective action** an intervention designed to solve a problem

**Due diligence** reasonable precautions taken to ensure that a business complies with the law

---

# Complete records to show that procedures are working

The HACCP system can seem a bit complicated, especially for smaller businesses. With this in mind, the Food Standards Agency (FSA) has developed a food safety management system to make it very simple and straightforward. It is called **Safer food, better business (SFBB)** for England and Wales. It comprises information packs, which are easy to read, with clearly labelled pictures and charts to fill in.

**Key term**

Safer food, better business (SFBB) an example of a food safety management system

SAFE METHOD:

## OPENING AND CLOSING CHECKS

**It is essential that you and your staff do certain checks every time you open and close. This helps you maintain the basic standards you need to make sure that your business makes food safely.**

| OPENING CHECKS |
| --- |
| **You should do these checks at the beginning of the day. You can also add your own checks to the list.** |
| Your fridges, chilled display equipment and freezers are working properly. |
| Your other equipment (e.g. oven) is working properly. |
| Staff are fit for work and wearing clean work clothes. |
| Food preparation areas are clean and disinfected, where appropriate (work surfaces, equipment, utensils etc.) |
| There are plenty of handwashing and cleaning materials (soap, paper towels, cloths etc.) |
| |
| |
| |

| CLOSING CHECKS |
| --- |
| **You should do these checks at the end of the day. You can also add your own checks to the list.** |
| No food is left out. |
| Food past its 'use by' date has been thrown away. |
| Dirty cloths have been removed for cleaning and replaced with clean ones. |
| Waste has been removed and new bags put into the bins. |
| |
| |
| |

 The opening and closing checks are also listed in the diary.

▲ **Safe method: opening and closing checks**

SAFE METHOD:

**EXTRA CHECKS**

Carrying out extra checks regularly helps you make sure your methods are being followed.

▲ **The SFBB food safety management system includes forms for extra checks**

There are two main parts. The first deals with safe methods such as avoiding cross-contamination, personal hygiene, cleaning, chilling and cooking. The second covers opening and closing checks, proving that methods are safe, recording safe methods, training records, supervision, stock control and the selection of suppliers.

The illustration here shows the form used to record opening and closing checks. This must be completed every day. It should take only a few minutes to fill in, and any problems must be recorded on this form.

As well as the opening and closing checks, other extra checks need to be carried out regularly, such as scheduled cleaning (for example weekly defrosting and cleaning of the fridge) or checking that the temperature probe is working correctly. Space is also provided to include additional checks so that businesses can personalise the forms for their own premises.

Food businesses must complete a food safety management booklet, either online or as a paper copy.

## Activity

Below is a list of control measures to produce safe food.

At https://www.food.gov.uk/business-guidance/safer-food-better-business-sfbb, you can find links to SFBB. Using this food management system and the list below, place each control measure in the correct box under the appropriate heading.

- Use reliable and trustworthy suppliers.
- No food to be kept after its 'use by' date.
- Cool food quickly.
- Store cooked foods above raw foods in the fridge.
- Cook food to 75°C.
- Clean work surfaces before use.
- Store frozen food at -18°C or below.
- Check delivery vehicles are clean.

- Make sure that food is transported at the correct temperatures.
- Check that chilled storage is ideally between 0°C and below 5°C.
- Avoid touching food with bare hands – use gloves or tongs.
- Use colour-coded equipment when preparing food to avoid cross-contamination.

Your teacher may give you a worksheet to help you and ask you to write these control measures in the correct place.

### Extension activity

Use the internet to find out which different types of equipment and materials can be colour coded, then explain how this can help to prevent cross-contamination.

## Knowledge check

1 What does HACCP stand for?
2 Give an example of a food safety hazard.
3 Explain what a critical limit is in a food safety management plan.

4 Why is it essential for food businesses to keep a record of their food safety management plan?

## Identify any critical control points and ensure that risks are removed or reduced to safe levels

In the following case study, you will be able to identify the critical control points and then either remove the risks or reduce them to a safe level. Read the case study carefully before you begin to complete the HACCP document.

## Case study

# Hazard analysis: egg mayonnaise and cucumber sandwich

### Method of preparation
Prepare, chill and serve cold

### Product details
This sandwich consists of hard-boiled egg, cucumber and mayonnaise. The sandwich is made to order and served unwrapped on a plate.

### Types of hazard
Biological – harmful bacteria.

Physical – objects that drop into the food, for example human hair.

Chemical contamination - from cleaning materials in the kitchen.

Food allergens – from other foods stored or prepared in the kitchen.

### Method of production
The eggs are boiled and chilled in the fridge the day before consumption; the cucumber is prepared on the day of service.

The sandwiches are made up to order on white bread.

### Premises
A small café serving lunches and homemade cakes.

There is one fridge and one freezer.

There is one food storage area for the ambient ingredients such as bread, flour, sugar and walnuts.

### Staff
All staff have received food hygiene training and hygiene awareness is good.

A new member of staff started work this week and will be given her food hygiene training next week, as this was the first course available.

### Problem
A customer in the café ordered an egg sandwich but, within a few minutes of eating it, developed itching and swelling of their face. They carried their own EpiPen, which they used, and this stopped the reaction very quickly.

### Questions
1   Complete the HACCP document below.

| Process step | Hazards | Control points |
|---|---|---|
| Delivery | Biological contamination of the eggs and cucumber <br> Incorrect temperature control | |
| Storage | Incorrect temperature control of the eggs and cucumber <br> Cross-contamination of ingredients in store cupboard <br> Nuts, flour and bread are all stored together | |
| Pre-preparation | Growth of harmful bacteria in eggs <br> Not washing the cucumber thoroughly <br> No washing of equipment between use with different ingredients | |
| Storage | Growth of harmful bacteria in eggs after cooking | |
| Serving | Growth of harmful bacteria if stored at room temperature for too long <br> Use of same tongs or gloves for serving different foods, for example sandwiches and cakes | |

2   Identify three critical control points (the most important control points you have identified).

3   Why is staff training so important for food handlers?

4   What actions should be taken if something goes wrong?

5   How could this incident have been prevented? Think about the storage of the ingredients and the serving of the sandwich.

# Practice questions

1 List **three** potential risks to health and security for a customer. (3 marks)

2 Health and safety is extremely important in the hospitality and catering industry. The data below shows the most common accidents that occur in the workplace.

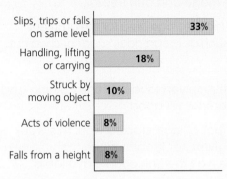

*Source*: www.hse.gov.uk/statistics/overall/hssh2021.pdf

   a  Explain how the Health and Safety at Work Act of 1974 can protect an employee. (4 marks)

   b  Explain how the Manual Handling Operations Regulations protect an employee. (2 marks)

   c  What does COSHH stand for? (1 mark)

3 State why this picture shows how to use a machine to cut meat safely. (2 marks)

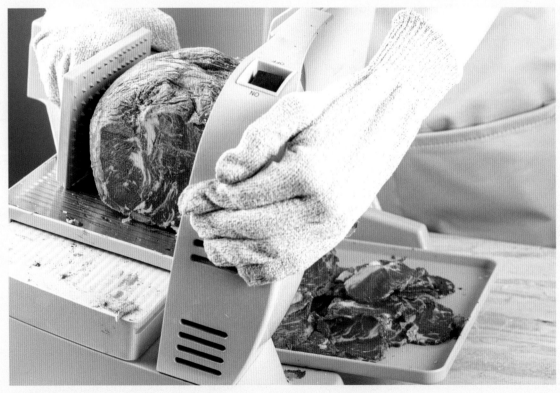

4  a  State the purpose of a Food Safety Management System. (2 marks)

   b  Explain why these documents are so important for food businesses. (4 marks)

5 Explain why food safety training is important for all staff from their very first day of work. (2 marks)

# 1.4 Food safety in hospitality and catering

## Getting started

Working with a partner, discuss all the ways you can think of that food can become contaminated to complete the following diagram.

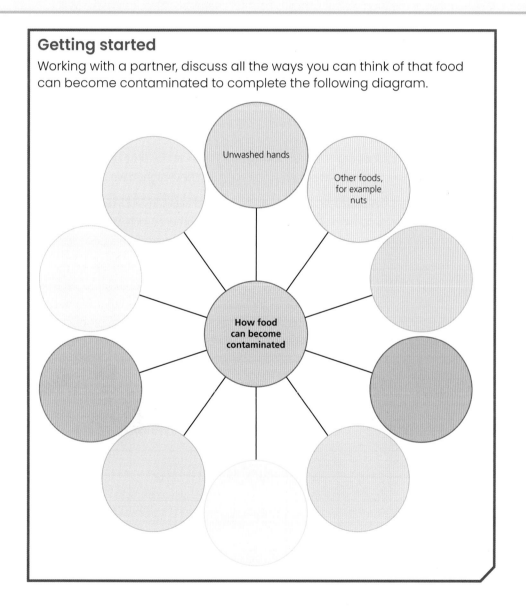

# 1.4.1 Food-related causes of ill health

We need to eat food to stay alive, but sometimes the foods we eat can make us ill.

There are different reasons for this. Listed below are some ways that foods can make us ill.

- Allergies: if we eat a food we are allergic to, our body reacts to it. This reaction can be very mild or very serious – sometimes so serious that it can cause death. Substances (including food) that cause allergies are known as allergens.
- Food intolerance: if we eat a food that our body finds difficult to digest, it can cause our body to have an unpleasant reaction.
- Bacteria: if the food we eat contains pathogenic (harmful) bacteria, it can make us ill.
- Chemicals: if the food we eat contains harmful chemicals, these can make us ill.

## Allergies

**Key terms**

**Allergy** a food allergy is when a person's body reacts in a negative way to a food they have eaten

**Allergen** a substance (for example food) that causes an allergic reaction

Food **allergies** can begin at different ages. There is no cure for food allergies, but children can sometimes grow out of them.

The best way to avoid an allergic reaction is to remove the allergy-causing food from our diet. We should always check food labels and ask staff when we're eating out to make sure we don't accidentally eat any **allergens**. Often, at the time of ordering, food service staff will ask customers about any food allergies they might have.

The UK government has produced a list of 14 known food allergens and, by law, these must be declared on food labels. In addition, food establishments such as restaurants and cafés must make sure customers know which of these allergens are in the foods served.

It is very important that the chefs making the food and the waiting staff are aware of the 14 allergens. The Food Standards Agency (FSA) is a government-controlled department that provides useful resources for food businesses to help them to track these allergens. The checklist presented here is an example of a resource produced by the FSA to help track the allergens in recipes.

| Allergens / Dish | Cereals containing gluten | Crustaceans | Dairy products | Eggs | Fish | Fruit and vegetables | Lupin | Molluscs |
|---|---|---|---|---|---|---|---|---|
| Feta salad | ✓ | | ✓ | ✓ | | ✓ | | |
| | | | | | | | | |
| | | | | | | | | |

▲ **A checklist to identify allergens in food**

Let's take a closer look at the 14 food allergens, in addition to some other foods that people may be allergic to.

Table 1.19 **Food allergens**

| Name of food allergen | Examples of foods containing this allergen | Image |
|---|---|---|
| Cereals containing gluten | Wheat, rye, oats, barley | |
| Crustaceans | Crab, lobster | |
| Dairy products | Milk, cheese, yoghurt, cream | |
| Eggs | Omelettes, quiche, cakes | |
| Fish | Oily fish, for example salmon, mackerel<br>White fish, for example haddock, cod | |
| Fruit and vegetables | Strawberries, kiwi, beetroot, carrot | |
| Lupin | Baked products containing lupin flour | |

| Name of food allergen | Examples of foods containing this allergen | Image |
|---|---|---|
| Molluscs | Scallops, oysters | |
| Mustard | Wholegrain mustard, Dijon mustard, English mustard, salad dressings, sauces | |
| Nuts | Including walnuts, hazelnuts, cashew nuts | |
| Peanuts | Salted peanuts, peanut butter, cakes, biscuits | |
| Sesame seeds | On baked products, such as bread rolls, sushi | |
| Soya | Soya beans, replacement meat products, dairy replacements | |
| Sulphur dioxide | Dried fruits, fruit juices, wine | |
| Wheat | Bread, cakes, biscuits containing wheat flour | |

In the UK, food allergens are monitored and assessed by experts. They give advice on which foods need to be labelled on pre-packed food. Businesses must emphasise these allergens, for example by writing the allergens in **bold** or CAPITALS or highlighting them on a menu. A new law was introduced in the UK in October 2021 making it a legal requirement for food businesses that make and package food before it is sold to include a full ingredients label. The law was introduced following the death of a teenager who bought and ate a baguette that contained sesame seeds, which were not included on the food product's label and were hidden within the bread. This new, stronger law will protect people with allergies and enable them to have greater confidence in the food they buy.

# Food intolerance

As well as food allergies, there is a condition known as **food intolerance**. This means that, when eaten, certain foods may produce unpleasant side effects such as bloating and other digestive problems.

Table 1.20 lists some substances in foods to which people may be intolerant.

**Table 1.20 Some examples of food intolerances**

| Name of food/substance | What is it? | Examples of foods containing this | Image |
|---|---|---|---|
| Gluten | The protein found in some cereals | Wheat, rye, oats, barley | |
| Lactose | A sugar found naturally in milk | Milk, cheese, yoghurt, cream | |
| Aspartame | An artificial sweetener | Diet drinks, desserts | |
| MSG | A flavour enhancer | Instant noodles, dried soups, stock cubes | |

Although food intolerances aren't as severe as allergies, if you have a food intolerance it is recommended that all labels are checked and the substances in question avoided to make sure all foods eaten can be digested properly. It is important to remember that, unlike allergens, the presence of these foods won't be indicated by highlighting or being written in bold as they are not all on the UK government's list of the 14 main allergens. Therefore, it is important that customers read food labels and, in the hospitality and catering industry, that waiting staff know the ingredients in each dish so they can pass this information on to customers.

| Key terms | 🔑 |
|---|---|

**Key terms**

**Bacteria** single-celled micro-organisms; some types of bacteria can cause food poisoning

**Pathogenic** harmful bacteria that can cause food poisoning

**Dehydration** (in people) when the body loses more water than it takes in

**Neutral foods** foods with a pH of around 7

# Bacteria

**Bacteria** are single-celled micro-organisms. Bacteria can be found everywhere around you: on your skin, in food, in soil, in water and in the air.

Most bacteria are harmless, but some are **pathogenic** and can cause food poisoning. General food poisoning symptoms are vomiting (being sick), nausea (feeling sick), diarrhoea, stomach pain and **dehydration**. (There is more information about pathogenic bacteria in section 1.4.2.)

Other types of bacteria cause food to decay; these are called food spoilage bacteria, and cause food to smell bad and lose its texture and flavour. Bacteria grow best with warmth (around body temperature, 37°C), and they prefer moist conditions on **neutral foods** containing protein. Examples of moist, neutral foods containing protein are meat, fish, poultry, gravy, egg dishes and seafood.

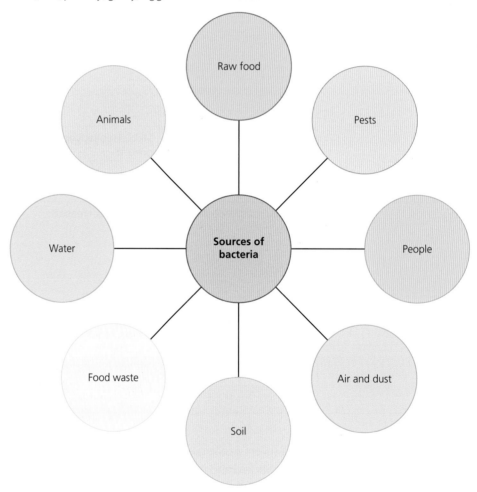

▲ **Main sources of bacteria**

## 1.4 Food safety in hospitality and catering

Table 1.21 lists the names of some harmful, or pathogenic, bacteria.

Bacteria have lots of different names and are found in many different places (sources). The 'special points' column on the right of the table gives more information about each type of bacteria.

**Table 1.21 Bacteria**

| Names of harmful (pathogenic) bacteria | Source – where do these bacteria come from? | Special points |
|---|---|---|
| *Bacillus cereus* | Cooked rice and pasta dishes<br>Meat and vegetable dishes<br>Dairy products<br>Soups, sauces<br>Sweet pastry products<br>Cereals and cereal products<br>Dust and soil<br> | Usually these foods have not been cooled, stored or reheated correctly.<br>During cooling time, after cooking, the **spores** will produce bacteria.<br>Bacteria can multiply quickly at these warm temperatures and produce **toxins** that are not destroyed by further reheating.<br>Only a small number of bacteria are needed to cause illness. |
| *Campylobacter* | Raw meat, raw poultry<br>Milk and milk products<br>Birds can contaminate food by pecking it and with their droppings<br>Inadequately pasteurised milk<br>Contaminated water supplies<br> | The most common cause of bacterial food poisoning in the UK.<br>Fewer than 500 *Campylobacter* bacteria are needed to cause infection.<br>*Campylobacter* bacteria are destroyed by heat. |
| *Clostridium perfringens* | Healthy animals and people – it is naturally carried in the intestines of animals and humans<br>Raw meat<br>Soil from root vegetables<br>Dust<br>Sewage and manure<br> | Can occur when food, usually meat, is prepared in advance and kept warm for several hours before serving.<br>*Clostridium perfringens* can reproduce during slow cooling and unrefrigerated storage.<br>Handwashing after visiting the toilet and after handling raw meat is very important.<br>Food should be kept out of the temperature danger zone and **anaerobic** conditions should be avoided. Anaerobic conditions could include being tightly sealed in a container or in a sealed plastic bag, as *Clostridium perfringens* only grows in anaerobic conditions (that is, without oxygen).<br>Spores can survive low temperatures.<br>When consumed it produces a toxin that causes illness. |

| Names of harmful (pathogenic) bacteria | Source – where do these bacteria come from? | Special points |
|---|---|---|
| *E. coli* | Raw and undercooked meats<br>Raw poultry<br>Untreated milk, water and dairy products<br>The intestines of animals and humans | Just a small number of *E. coli* bacteria can cause illness.<br>The bacteria can survive refrigeration and freezer storage.<br>Thorough cooking of food and **pasteurisation** will destroy it. |
| *Listeria* | Cook-chill foods (foods that have been cooked, then chilled and stored in the fridge), for example ready meals<br>Untreated dairy foods, pâté, smoked fish<br>Soil<br>Sewage<br>Water<br>Animals and people | *Listeria* can grow at low temperatures and will multiply in fridges at 5°C.<br>It is destroyed by cooking food thoroughly and by the process of pasteurisation.<br>Pregnant people, babies, those with a weakened immune system and the elderly (**vulnerable groups**) are most at risk.<br>Listeria infections during pregnancy can cause miscarriage or premature delivery.<br>Vulnerable groups should avoid eating unpasteurised dairy products.<br>Salads and raw vegetables should be washed before eating. |
| *Salmonella* | Eggs<br>Poultry<br>Cooked meats<br>Unpasteurised milk<br>Insects and sewage<br>Intestines of farm animals and people<br>Pets and rodents | *Salmonella* is infectious (it can be passed from person to person easily).<br>Avoid drinking water from untreated sources.<br>It is destroyed by cooking. |
| *Staphylococcus aureus* | Raw milk<br>Meat and meat products<br>People – *staphylococcus aureus* can live on the skin, in the nose or on the fingers of some infected people | Cross-contamination occurs when an infected person handles ready-to-eat foods.<br>Storage of infected foods at room temperature before consumption allows the bacteria to multiply and produce a harmful toxin.<br>High standards of personal hygiene are essential. |

# Harmful chemicals in food

Foods may be contaminated by chemical substances such as:

- cleaning fluids
- insecticides
- bleach.

These chemicals are extremely poisonous if swallowed.

Poisoning with these chemicals often occurs when they have been moved from their original labelled container to different container and may then be mistaken for another substance. It is essential that chemicals such as these are kept in their original containers and stored in a safe place away from children and foods.

Key terms

**Spore** a dormant form of bacteria able to survive when food storage conditions are not ideal

**Toxin** a poison, especially one produced by micro-organisms such as bacteria

**Anaerobic** a process that does not require oxygen

**Pasteurisation** the process of prolonging the keeping quality of products such as milk by heating it to 72°C for 15 seconds to destroy most harmful bacteria

**Vulnerable groups** groups of people who are more at risk of health issues, for example the very old and the very young

▲ **Chemicals should be kept in their original containers and never stored near food**

# Food labelling laws

Food labelling regulations make sure that the correct information is provided to customers about food sold in shops, cafés, restaurants and other catering establishments.

Food labels provide information that helps people to:

- make careful decisions about the food they choose to buy
- store and cook the food they choose to buy correctly, to prevent food-related causes of ill health
- find out the nutrient content of food and how it contributes to their daily food needs.

▲ **Labelling on the front of foods is not legally required in the UK, but many supermarkets use the traffic light system on the front of ready-to-eat foods**

# What information is needed on a food label?

There are laws that have to be followed by all food producers. This is to make sure that food labelling is controlled and clear to everyone. All food producers must follow these rules and must not mislead consumers.

Labels must be clear, easy to read and understand, and must never mislead. Labels must include:

- the name of the food
- an ingredients list
- any ingredients that may cause allergies or intolerances
- weight or volume
- a date of minimum durability (a 'use by' or 'best before' date)
- the storage conditions needed
- the name and address of the food manufacturer
- country of origin
- alcoholic strength by volume (if relevant)
- instructions for use
- nutrition information.

## The name of the food

The name of the food cannot be false or misleading. It should be precise enough that customers know exactly what it is. For example, a tart would be labelled with its main flavour (for example, a cheese and onion tart).

## Ingredients list

Ingredients must be listed in descending order by weight: this means the ingredient that is the heaviest is listed first and the ingredient that is the lightest is listed last.

If any ingredients have been changed – say, dried apricots are used instead of fresh ones – this should be clearly indicated on the label.

## Ingredients that may cause allergies or intolerances

It is really important that customers read ingredients labels when choosing foods or menu items to check if a food is safe for them to eat.

An allergen is a substance that can cause an allergic reaction in some people (see page 84). The law states that allergens must be highlighted or emphasised in some way in the main ingredients list on product labels.

An allergen advice warning may be given if there is a chance that an ingredient may have come into contact with any other potentially allergenic ingredients.

## The weight or volume of the food

Food labels must state the quantity of food in the pack – its weight or volume and, if applicable, the number of items.

### Ingredients:

Dried and sweetened dried fruit (25%) [sultanas, sweetened dried pineapple (10%) (sugar, pineapple, acid: citric acid, preservative: **sulphur dioxide**), dates, raisins], **barley** flakes, **oat** flakes, **wheat** flakes, toasted and malted **wheat** flakes (**wheat**, **barley** malt extract).

### Allergy advice

For allergens, see ingredients in bold. May contain nuts and milk.

▲ **Allergen label**

▲ **Food labels must state the quantity of the food**

### A date of minimum durability (a 'use by' or 'best before' date)

'Use by' dates are usually given on perishable foods that require refrigeration, such as fresh meat, cheese and ready-to-eat foods. Such foods should be eaten before this date to prevent food poisoning.

'Best before' dates are usually given on foods that keep for longer, such as dried or canned foods, biscuits or breakfast cereals. Foods should be eaten before this date for quality reasons. Biscuits, for example, may be eaten after this date but their quality may be reduced – they may taste stale and/or have gone soft.

Some people are surprised that eggs have a 'best before' date, rather than a 'use by' date. These are the exception to the rule, however, and should be consumed before their 'best before' date as they are a food poisoning risk.

### Storage conditions needed

Storage conditions need to be given to ensure the food is stored safely. For example, a product may state 'once opened, store in the fridge and consume within three days'. Alternatively, it may state 'suitable for home freezing'.

### Name and address of the food manufacturer

The name and address of the manufacturer must be included on the food label in case a customer wishes to contact them, particularly if they have a complaint about the food.

### Country of origin

The label must state clearly where the product has come from, for example 'Country of origin: Spain'.

▲ **The country of origin must be shown on the label**

### Alcoholic strength by volume (if relevant)

When a product or drink contains more than 1.2 per cent alcohol, this must be indicated on the label.

## Instructions for use

The instructions for use must be detailed enough to make sure the food product can be prepared or cooked correctly. The required time and temperature of cooking must be given in the case of raw poultry and meat.

We keep to our own special, trusted recipe and a blend of the finest ingredients to make sure this rich, classic soup remains a firm family favourite. Perfect with warm crusty bread. Sensational with a splash of sherry.

**COOKING INSTRUCTIONS**

**HOB:** Empty contents into a saucepan and stir gently while heating. Do not boil or overcook as this will impair the flavour.

**MICROWAVE (Category E - 850W):** Microwave ovens vary. The following is a guide only. Empty contents into a microwaveable container and cover. Heat on full power for 2 minutes. Stir, then heat for a further 1 minute. Check that product is hot before serving.

**INGREDIENTS**

Water, Concentrated Tomato, Wheat Flour, Cornflour, Oxtails (1%), Sugar, Onion Powder, Colour, Yeast Extracts, Salt, Garlic Salt

**CONTAINS**

Gluten, Wheat

**NUTRITION INFORMATION**

| Typical Values | Per 100g | Per serving (200g) |
|---|---|---|
| Energy | 158kJ /37kcal | 315kJ /75kcal |
| Protein | 1.6g | 3.3g |
| Carbohydrate (of which sugars) | 6.5g (1.7g) | 13.1g (3.4g) |
| Fat (of which saturates) | 0.5g (0.2g) | 1.0g (0.4g) |
| Fibre | 0.3g | 0.6g |
| Sodium | 0.3g | 0.5g |

▲ **Food labels must show how to prepare the food correctly**

## Nutrition information

By law, all foods must have the nutrient content of the product stated clearly on the label.

Nutritional information must be given per 100 g or 100 ml and can also be given per serving.

Information on the following has to be provided:
- energy (in kilojoules and kilocalories)
- fat (in grams)
- saturated fat (in grams)
- carbohydrates (in grams)
- sugars (in grams)
- protein (in grams)
- salt (in grams).

Voluntary nutritional information is sometimes included such as fibre, vitamins and minerals.

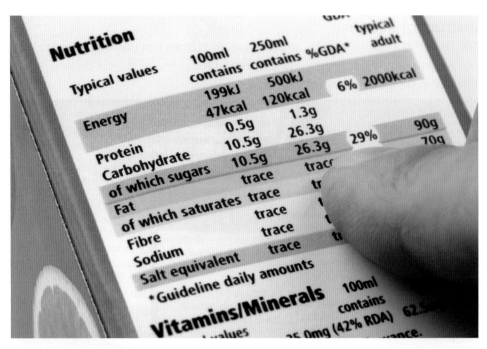

▲ **Nutritional values are also often given per serving**

Information on the front of the pack is voluntary, but many manufacturers and supermarkets use traffic light labelling, especially on pre-packed meals.

Traffic light labels show whether a product has high (red), medium (amber) or low (green) amounts of energy, fat, saturates, sugars and salt.

We should try to eat more greens and ambers, and fewer reds.

The reference intake (RI) is a guide to the maximum amount of fat, saturates, sugar and salt that an adult should eat every day.

| Energy | Sugar | Fat | Saturates | Salt |
|---|---|---|---|---|
| 1046kJ 250kcal | 5g | 15g | 6g | 0.2g |
| 15% | 18% | 2% | 39% | 19% |

% of adult's reference intake. Typical values per 100g: Energy 4530kJ/750kcal

▲ **Traffic light labelling can help the consumer make healthier choices; this label shows how much of the reference intake (as a percentage) this product provides per serving**

## Activity

Stick a food label in the centre of a sheet of A3 paper and identify all of the information shown on the label.

Your teacher may give you a food label with arrows pointing to each piece of information it includes to help you. Using the list on page 95, label each arrow with the correct piece of information.

### Extension activity

Label or highlight any additional information given, such as health claims or serving suggestions. Why do you think food manufacturers include this additional information?

# Food safety regulations

These food safety regulations apply to food businesses and cover all activities involving food. The rules in these regulations clearly set out the responsibility of food businesses to:

> … produce food safely and make sure it is consistently safe to eat; food is unsafe if it is harmful to health and unfit for human consumption; keep records of suppliers so that food can be traced; businesses must withdraw food that does not meet food safety requirements.

The whole food chain, from **farm to fork**, is covered by legislation. Farm to fork means that food can be traced through all the stages of production, processing and distribution back to its original source.

These regulations require that food is stored, handled, cooked and served safely, that premises are clean and hygienic, and that the people handling food follow basic hygiene rules.

## Key term

**Farm to fork** a strategy that allows food to be traced through all stages of production back to the original source

## Food Safety Act

This act is concerned with all aspects of food production and sale. It affects everyone involved in the production, processing, storage, distribution and sale of food.

The main purpose of the Food Safety Act is to make sure that food is safe to eat. If food handlers do not do everything in their power to make sure food is safe to eat, they are breaking the law.

▲ **Everyone who handles food must follow the Food Safety Act**

▲ **Food must be safe to eat**

Anyone who produces or sells food must not add any substance to food or put food through any process or treatment that could make it harmful to health.

People called Environmental Health Officers (EHOs) work for the government and can inspect food premises at any reasonable time. During these inspections, they carefully check the premises and practices to make sure food is prepared, cooked and stored correctly. If there is a problem, the business' owner or manager has to correct it, to make sure the food is safe to eat. See page 110 for further information on the role of EHOs.

The Food Safety Act also provides a defence for food producers, processors and retailers. They must prove that all reasonable precautions have been taken to prevent a food safety incident. If a problem does occur and they can prove that all reasonable precautions were taken, they can be let off a food safety offence. For this to occur, they would need to be able to provide details of their **food safety management systems** and plans, and evidence to show that they had followed these requirements (see pages 75–80).

If the requirements of the Food Safety Act are not followed, businesses owners or managers can be taken to court and fined, or even sent to prison.

> ### Key term
>
> **Food safety management system** practical steps to identify and control hazards in order to establish and maintain food safety

## Knowledge check

1  Name the four main food-related causes of ill health.
2  There are 14 food allergens recognised by the UK government; name five of these.
3  Gluten is both an allergen and a cause of food intolerance. Name four foods that contain gluten.
4  Describe the four ideal conditions most bacteria require to multiply.
5  Name three pathogenic bacteria and give a food source for each.
6  An ingredients list must be shown on a food label. Explain why this is important.
7  Why is regular handwashing important before preparing food?
8  Explain the differences between a 'use by' date and a 'best before' date.
9  What is the main purpose of the Food Safety Act?

## 1.4.2 Symptoms and signs of food-induced ill health

## How bacteria make you ill

Pathogenic bacteria are harmful bacteria that can cause illness. Illness can occur as a result of eating too many bacteria that have been allowed to multiply in food – for instance, if the food has not been handled or stored correctly.

Most types of food poisoning require the consumption of thousands of bacteria. *E. coli*, however, requires the consumption of only a few of these types of bacteria to cause serious illness. Some types of bacteria enter the stomach and intestine, and then they multiply inside the body; this is how *Campylobacter* and *Salmonella* cause illness.

## Symptoms of food poisoning

A symptom is a sign or indication of a disease or illness. If someone unknowingly **ingests** bacteria or toxins, their body will react by developing symptoms such as diarrhoea, vomiting, stomach pain, headaches and/or sweating. Some of these symptoms are visible and some non-visible.

The symptoms of food poisoning can begin immediately (for example, in the case of anaphylactic shock) or develop several days after exposure.

Tables 1.22 and 1.23 list possible visible and non-visible symptoms, respectively. Some people may have only one symptom, while others may have several.

> **Key term**
>
> **Ingest** take (food, drink or another substance) into the body by swallowing or absorbing it

Table 1.22 **Visible symptoms**

| Visible symptoms | Description |
| --- | --- |
| Anaphylactic shock | This is a rare but very serious allergic reaction and can cause death.<br>It affects the whole body and can include the following symptoms:<br>■ swelling of the throat and mouth<br>■ difficulty breathing<br>■ confusion<br>■ blue lips or skin<br>■ collapse and loss of consciousness.<br>Anaphylactic shock is a medical emergency that requires immediate treatment. People who are known to have severe allergies likely to trigger anaphylactic shock should carry an EpiPen with them; this contains a substance called adrenaline, which helps to control their symptoms until more specialist treatment can be given. |
| Bloating | This is when a person's stomach is stretched. It might feel puffy and uncomfortable. |
| Breathing difficulties | For instance, fast or shallow breathing. |
| Chills | Chills are when a person feels cold and their body may shiver. |
| Diarrhoea | Diarrhoea is the frequent passing of watery or loose stools (poo). |
| Facial swelling | A swollen and/or puffy face. |
| Pale or sweating skin | When the skin becomes much lighter in colour and feels sticky. |
| Rash | An area of irritated or swollen skin. Some rashes are itchy, red or painful. |
| Vomiting | When the contents of the stomach are forced up and out through the mouth. |
| Weight loss | A decrease in body weight. |

▲ An EpiPen is used to treat anaphylactic shock, a severe allergic reaction to a food

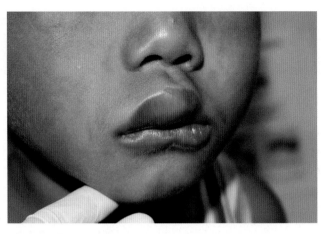

▲ Facial swelling

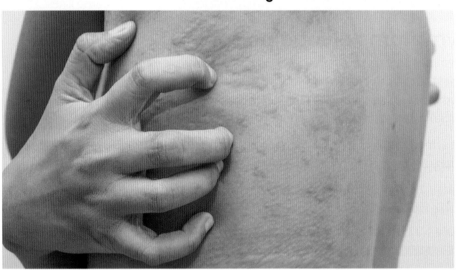

▲ A hives-type rash

Table 1.23 **Non-visible symptoms**

| Non-visible symptoms | Description |
| --- | --- |
| Constipation | When bowel movements become less frequent and stools are also more difficult to pass. |
| Feeling sick | Nausea. An unsettled feeling in the stomach. Thinking about food makes it worse. |
| Painful joints | Pain and discomfort caused by swelling of the joint tissue. |
| Stomach ache | A pain in the tummy/belly area. |
| Weakness | When the body feels tired. Some parts of the body may not move properly. |
| Wind/flatulence | When gas builds up in the digestive system. |

## Knowledge check

1   How should anaphylactic shock be treated?

## 1.4.3 Preventative control measures of food-induced ill health

# Cross-contamination

**Cross-contamination** is the process by which a substance that is dirty or harmful spreads from one place to another. It can occur at any stage of food production – it often involves the transfer of bacteria from contaminated foods (usually raw) to **ready-to-eat foods**. This can include direct contact (for example raw meat touching cooked meat), or via dripping and indirect contact. With drip contact, for example, the juices from a raw chicken could drip on to ready-to-eat food, such as a cooked meat pie, and contaminate it with harmful bacteria. Indirect contact could be in the form of bacteria being spread from either unwashed hands handling both raw and cooked foods, or someone using the same equipment for raw and cooked foods.

It is safest to always assume that all sources of bacteria (for example hands, raw foods, insects, used equipment) are contaminated with harmful bacteria.

**Key terms**

**Cross-contamination** the process by which a substance that is dirty or harmful spreads from one place to another

**Ready-to-eat foods** foods that require no further cooking or reheating

▲ **Cross-contamination is when harmful bacteria pass on to ready-to-eat foods**

To prevent cross-contamination, either the sources of the harmful substance should be removed or preventions put in place to stop the harmful substance from spreading. The handling of food should be kept to a minimum; for example, tongs could be used to pick up food rather than hands, and hand contact with surfaces such as taps could be replaced with elbow-operated or electronic taps, to reduce the number of surfaces that hands come into contact with.

▲ **Elbow taps can help to prevent cross-contamination**

To further prevent cross-contamination, a 'clean as you go' approach should be used, to make sure all cleaning is carried out as and when any contamination occurs.

Food-induced ill health can be caused by pathogenic bacteria, allergens, foods which cause intolerances and chemicals (see pages 84–90). Preventing the spread of harmful substances on to food via cross-contamination is very important, as for some people being exposed to certain food allergens can cause death.

The use of colour coding in the kitchen helps to prevent cross-contamination. This means that different types of food are prepared on different-coloured chopping boards. This stops bacteria from raw food being transferred on to cooked, ready-to-eat food. Any food that is cooked and ready to eat should be protected from contact with raw foods. There are normally a lot of bacteria in raw food but, once it has been cooked, most of them are destroyed. If the cooked food then comes into contact with raw food, however, this puts it at risk of becoming contaminated. To prevent the spread of food allergens, the use of purple chopping boards is becoming more common. These are used to prepare foods for people who are avoiding allergens such as wheat and nuts.

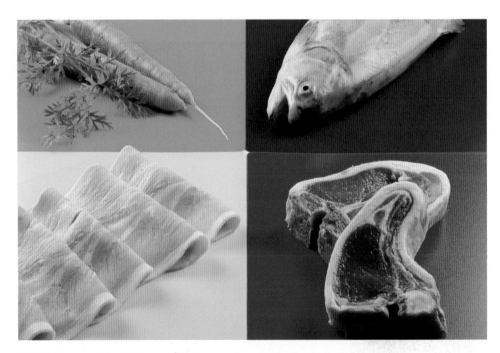

▲ **Colour-coded chopping boards can help to prevent cross-contamination**

# Correct temperature in delivery, storage, preparation and service

It is very important that food is kept at the correct temperature (temperature control). Many outbreaks of food poisoning are caused by ready-to-eat foods being kept for too long within the **temperature danger zone**.

# What is the temperature danger zone?

The temperature danger zone is the range of temperatures between 5°C and 63°C at which bacteria can multiply.

- Bacteria grow very slowly or do not grow at all at temperatures below 5°C.
- No bacteria can grow at temperatures above 63°C.
- Bacteria will multiply the fastest at around body temperature, that is 37°C.

The temperature danger zone does not apply to non-perishable foods, which are normally stored in cupboards at around 17–20°C.

# Temperature control of high-risk foods

High-risk foods are those ready-to-eat foods that are most likely to cause food poisoning.

The basic principles of temperature control of high-risk foods are to:

- keep hot food hot, at 63°C or above
- keep cold food cold, below 5°C
- keep prepared food out of the temperature danger zone of 5–63°C.

The following principles are important:

- fridge temperatures should be from 0°C to below 5°C
- the temperature danger zone is 5–63°C
- the safe reheating and cooking temperature is 75°C.

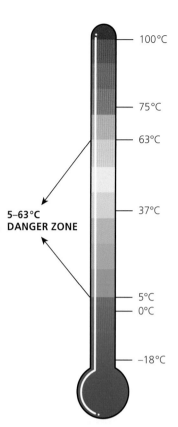

**5–63°C DANGER ZONE**

▲ **The temperature danger zone is 5–63°C**

▲ **Prawn cocktail is an example of a high-risk food that should be kept chilled**

A **temperature probe** is essential in a commercial kitchen to check that food temperatures are being met and held. It can be used to check that:

- food is properly defrosted before cooking, especially poultry and joints of meat
- cooked food has reached a safe temperature of 75°C or above
- ready-to-serve food is still hot (63°C or above)
- reheated food has reached at least 75°C — remember, food should only be reheated once.

**Key term**

**Temperature probe** a device used to check the internal temperature of food

▲ **A temperature probe is essential to monitor food temperatures**

# Perishable and non-perishable foods

**Perishable foods** are foods with a fairly short shelf life. They should usually be stored in the fridge or freezer. Examples of perishable foods are:

- raw meat and cooked meat
- poultry and fish
- milk and eggs
- butter, low-fat spread and yoghurts
- cheeses
- vegetables, fruits and salads.

▲ **Examples of perishable foods**

> **Key term**
>
> **Perishable foods** foods with a shorter shelf life (for example fresh meat), which are usually stored in the fridge

**Non-perishable foods** are foods that have been processed in some way to prevent the growth of micro-organisms and to prolong their shelf life. These foods are usually stored at an **ambient temperature** in food cupboards.

Such foods include:
- canned foods
- dried pasta and rice
- breakfast cereals
- flour
- coffee powder
- sugar.

**Key terms**

**Non-perishable foods** foods with a longer shelf life (for example breakfast cereals), which are usually kept at room temperature

**Ambient temperature** normal room temperature

▲ **Examples of non-perishable foods**

# Cooking of food

Some foods can safely be eaten raw, for example most fruits and vegetables once they have been washed or peeled.

Other foods, such as meat and poultry and most seafood, need to be cooked, not just to improve the texture and flavour of the food, but to kill harmful (pathogenic) bacteria that may cause food poisoning. Although it is possible to eat some meats rare (lightly cooked) – for example beef steak – other meat and poultry must be cooked right through to the middle to ensure that bacteria are destroyed and the food is safe to eat. For example, poultry should always be cooked through, until the juices run clear and the temperature is at least 75°C at the thickest point.

# Delivery

Food should be purchased from known, reliable and hygienic suppliers, and food deliveries should be made in clean, properly equipped vehicles with clean drivers wearing the appropriate protective clothing.

Depending on the types of food being delivered, delivery vans may also require refrigeration or freezers to transport the foods at the correct temperatures.

Deliveries should be checked on arrival. At first, a visual check should be made to ensure everything looks clean and fresh.

▲ **Poultry must be cooked thoroughly to destroy harmful bacteria**

Food should be suitably labelled and date-coded, and should have sufficient **shelf life** to enable it to be used. Any foods with damaged packaging or past their 'use by' or 'best before' dates should be rejected.

Temperature probes should be used to monitor and then record the temperature of foods on arrival. Chilled foods should be delivered at below 5°C, and frozen food at or below −18°C. However, the law states that chilled deliveries can be up to 8°C, which is the legal maximum temperature for chilled food. Any foods not meeting these temperatures should be rejected.

Delivery records should be completed, which includes the checks made, details of the checks (for example the temperatures recorded) and the name of the person completing the checks.

Once you are happy with the goods, they can then be taken to be stored. The foods delivered should be moved to storage within 15 minutes of unloading.

If there are regular problems with food deliveries, alternative suppliers will need to be found.

▲ **Food deliveries must be made in well-equipped, clean vehicles**

## Storage

Following delivery, foods should be stored at either ambient, chilled or freezer temperatures:

- ambient temperature = 17°C
- **chilled (fridge) temperature** = 0 to below 5°C
- **freezer temperature** = −18°C or below

During the storage process these foods must be kept in food containers, and away from any unfit food or chemicals.

### Chilled foods

As noted above, chilled foods should be stored at a temperature of 0 to below 5°C. Ideally, raw meat and poultry will be kept in a separate refrigerator operating at temperatures between −1°C and +1°C.

Cooked meat should always be stored above raw meat if they are kept in the same unit.

Eggs are stored by the retailer at an ambient temperature of below 20°C, however caterers should store eggs in the fridge at below 5°C. They may be removed from the fridge 30 minutes before cooking, depending on the recipe.

Milk and cream should be stored in the fridge.

Fruits and vegetables, once cut or peeled, should be chilled at 0 to below 5°C. Some fruits, such as bananas and pineapples, should be stored at between 10°C and 13°C to avoid chill damage.

### Frozen foods

Frozen foods should be kept at −18°C or below. This will ensure that bacteria cannot grow. Ice cream is the exception to this. It may be stored at −12°C before use to improve its texture for serving.

**Key terms**

**Shelf life** how long a food product lasts for before it starts to go bad

**Chilled (fridge) temperature** temperature of 0 to below 5°C

**Freezer temperature** temperature of −18°C or below

## Foods stored at ambient temperatures

Foods such as flour and cereals should be stored in a dry environment at below 20°C. These foods should be checked regularly for signs of insects or rodents.

Canned foods should also be stored in a cool and well-ventilated place. Once cans have been opened, their contents should be stored in a separate covered container and refrigerated. Cans should be checked weekly to make sure they are in good condition.

## Stock rotation

Stock rotation ensures that there is less food wastage and helps to prevent food poisoning. Daily checks should be made on any perishable foods being stored, and weekly checks on non-perishable foods.

It is very important to make sure you follow the first in, first out (FIFO) rule (see also page 49). This means that the food that is closest to its 'best before' or 'use by' date should be used first. For foods without date marks, such as fruits and vegetables, the food that has been stored for the longest time should be used first as long as it is still fresh. To assist with this, it is recommended that written stock control records are kept.

Before using foods, you should check they are within their 'best before' or 'use by' date, in good condition and well packaged.

# Preparation
## Defrosting food

Some foods – such as peas, chips, burgers, vegetables and fish – do not need to be defrosted before cooking as they are best cooked from frozen. Joints of meat, poultry and bulky food should be defrosted before use, to ensure they can be cooked in a reasonable amount of time and evenly. If such foods are not defrosted properly, their core temperature may not reach the 75°C needed to kill harmful (pathogenic) bacteria.

▲ **It is important to defrost poultry before cooking**

You can tell if food is properly defrosted as there will be no ice crystals (small grains of ice that can be seen or felt in food) remaining and the food will be soft. In the case of poultry, an extra check is to see if the legs and wings move freely.

### Checklist for defrosting raw frozen meat and poultry

1  Plan ahead and know how long defrosting will take (for example, large turkeys could take several days to defrost).
2  Defrost in a container, so the liquid is contained as it defrosts.
3  Cover the food that is defrosting.
4  Once the food is defrosted, cook it straight away.
5  Never refreeze defrosted food.

---

**Activity**

Design an information sheet for a Year 7 student to show them how to defrost a chicken safely. Use images if you prefer.

Your teacher may give you a piece of A4 paper with an image of a frozen chicken in the centre to help you. Label this to describe how the chicken should be defrosted safely.

**Key term**

**Antibacterial spray**
a spray designed
to destroy most
bacteria on work
surfaces

## Clean work surfaces

Work surfaces in kitchens should be kept clean so that they are free from bacteria. They should be cleaned before any food preparation takes place, during food preparation and at the end of the practical session.

Work surfaces should be cleaned with hot, soapy water using a clean cloth. An **antibacterial spray** should be used afterwards, which will destroy virtually all the bacteria on the work surface.

▲ **Food should be served at the correct temperature; avoid touching foods with your hands if possible**

## Service

Ideally, food should be served as soon as it has been cooked as this will ensure that bacteria have no time to grow. If this is not possible, the food should be cooled quickly and then chilled or frozen before being reheated later. Alternatively, food may be kept hot (at 63°C or above) before serving.

Food should be served using clean utensils, such as tongs or other implements, to avoid cross-contamination. You should avoid touching food while you are serving it, if this is possible. Plates should be the appropriate temperature for the food: cold if being used for cold food and hot if being used for hot food. This will help to ensure that food is kept out of the temperature danger zone.

# Physical contamination

Physical contamination is when objects end up in food that are not supposed to be there. This type of contamination can occur at any stage of food production. Physical contamination includes pieces of metal or plastic entering the food during production. Parts of the food product that should have been removed during processing, including pips, stones, shell, bones and stalks, can also contaminate the end product.

Physical contamination also includes fragments of food packaging or objects present as the result of careless food handling, such as plasters, jewellery and hair. Pests can also contaminate food with their droppings, saliva and urine.

▲ **You should be extra careful not to accidentally contaminate food if you're wearing a plaster**

## Knowledge check

1 Give two examples of how the cross-contamination of food may occur.
2 State the following key temperatures:
   a chilled (fridge) temperature
   b freezer temperature
   c temperature danger zone
   d minimum temperature for reheating food
   e minimum temperature for serving hot food.

## 1.4.4 The Environmental Health Officer (EHO)

As discussed on page 98, Environmental Health Officers (EHOs) are responsible for carrying out checks and implementing measures to protect public health, and providing support in order to minimise health and safety hazards.

There are many other aspects to their jobs, but their main role is to make sure that people have a better quality of life in a healthier and safer society.

EHOs are government employees who work for local councils in specialist areas such as food safety, health and safety at work, housing and environmental protection. For this course you will need to know about their role in monitoring the quality of the food we eat outside the home.

You will need to know and understand the role of the EHO and what their responsibilities are.

## Responsibilities

### Collecting evidence, including samples for testing, photographs and interviews

EHOs have the right to enter food premises at all reasonable hours and can visit without making an appointment. They may collect samples of food and take them away for testing. They may also take photographs and interview staff about the premises and their working practices. An EHO may take samples of food with them if there is a suspicion that food is contaminated and is likely to cause food poisoning or disease. Food that is taken away may be examined in a laboratory to find out if it is safe to eat.

In order to **condemn food**, EHOs must present their findings to a court. The court will consider the information and decide whether the food poses a risk to human health and whether the food should be destroyed.

**Key term**

**Condemned food** food that is unfit for human consumption

▲ **All areas of the kitchen must be inspected by the Environmental Health Officers**

# Enforcing environmental health laws and following up complaints

At the end of an inspection by an EHO, they will complete a report into their findings; this is left at the premises with the owner/manager. It will state which regulations (rules) have been broken and what action needs to be taken to meet the legal minimum requirements. It is likely that the EHO will visit again to check that the issues have been dealt with.

Sometimes customers may have made complaints about food premises, which are then followed up by the EHO. As in the case of routine inspection, if a regulation has been broken the EHO will follow up with information on any action that needs to be taken by the owner or manager.

# Following up outbreaks of food poisoning

If someone gets food poisoning, or reports what they think is food poisoning, from a food premises preparing or selling food, an EHO may be called in to inspect the premises.

The first priority of the EHO will be to find out whether or not the illness is caused by food and, if it is, prevent the spread of illness. In all cases of reported food poisoning, the EHO has the responsibility to find out if hygiene regulations or the Food Safety Act have not been followed. If the EHO believes there has been a **breach of legislation** they will start an investigation. Sometimes, the EHO may recommend that the premises is closed while an investigation is carried out.

**Key term**

**Breach of legislation** breaking the law

During the investigation, the EHO will find out which organism, or chemical, was responsible for the illness. They will try to trace all related cases of the food poisoning and carriers, especially those involved in food handling. The EHO will also find out at which stage of the food preparation process the bacteria were able to increase.

The EHO will recommend how food should be prepared in future to prevent the food poisoning happening again. It is important that details of all the people reported to be suffering symptoms of suspected food poisoning are collected as soon as possible. The EHO may ask that everyone involved in the preparation of the suspect food is tested to see if they are carrying certain bacteria. If anyone involved in the preparation of the suspect food reports symptoms, then they must not work in contact with food while the investigation is being carried out.

At the end of the outbreak, the EHO will analyse the results of the investigation and say what changes (if any) need to be made to how food is stored, prepared, cooled and/or served in the future.

## Inspecting businesses for food safety standards

EHOs regularly inspect food premises. These inspections may begin with a discussion with the manager or owner of the business to identify the hazards and risks, depending on the type of premises being inspected. During this discussion, the EHO will look at the staff involved, their training, and the type and quality of food being handled.

The EHO will wear suitable protective clothing to prevent them contaminating the food in any way. They will give verbal feedback on the inspection and ask questions to make sure that both the law and good practice are being followed. The EHO will look at the way the business operates and will identify potential hazards. They will inspect the food safety management system and plans to make sure they are relevant, up to date and reviewed regularly.

▲ An EHO inspecting a food premises

If the EHO identifies any problems, they will advise on what needs to change in the future. They will then complete a report of the findings of the inspection, which will tell the business what **enforcement action**, if any, needs to be taken. This may lead to risk assessments being updated or further staff training taking place.

## Giving evidence in prosecutions

Sometimes, owners or managers of food businesses break food safety laws and are prosecuted (taken to court). EHOs may be asked to give evidence in court about an offence and to say which laws have been broken.

The evidence given may include photographs or films of the premises and/or food samples, and evidence from customers or from laboratory reports.

The EHO would also state the nature of the contamination. For example:
- in the case of physical contamination they would describe the object, such as an insect or piece of metal, and its size and type
- a chemical contamination could be something like bleach in food
- a biological contamination could be, say, bacteria in food.

The EHO would also consider the impact on the health and well-being of customers, and the seriousness of the risks involved. They would say whether the offence was a one-off or part of a failure in systems and procedures.

The policies and procedures in place may also be used in a prosecution if they are thought to be unsuitable.

▲ **Environmental Health Officers are sometimes asked to give evidence in court**

## Maintaining evidence

It is important that the EHO keeps any evidence they gather safe, in case it is needed for use in a prosecution in court. Such evidence may include:

■ inspection notes – these should include the date, and should be presented in date order and signed

■ records of conversations and any emails, including dates and details of the people involved

■ photographs, with information as to who took them and when they were taken

■ food samples – kept at appropriate temperatures in suitable packaging, to avoid contamination.

## Submitting reports

At the end of the inspection, the EHO will complete a report into their inspection findings, which is left at the premises with the manager or owner. This report will state what enforcement action (if any) is needed. Enforcement action can range from simple verbal advice or an informal or formal letter and notices, through to prosecution (taking the business owner to court).

▲ **Environmental Health Officers write reports on their findings**

## Knowledge check

1 What is the main role of an Environmental Health Officer?

2 Why may Environmental Health Officers collect food samples from food premises?

3 Why is it important that Environmental Health Officers visit food premises regularly and without making an appointment?

4 Environmental Health Officers have an important job in terms of ensuring food safety. Describe how they may respond to an outbreak of food poisoning.

## Activity

1   Find out more about reactions to food allergens. Search YouTube for 'food allergens UK', and watch the following clips:
   ■ www.youtube.com/watch?v=S7CApLk9bwc
   ■ www.youtube.com/watch?v=fHo15_MxS4g
   Then visit the following website: www.nhs.uk/conditions/food-allergy
2   Make a PowerPoint presentation of your findings. Include information on the 14 food allergens and the symptoms these may produce.
3   Find up-to-date news stories on food allergens that demonstrate how serious reactions to foods (especially anaphylactic shock) may be.
4   Present your findings to your class.

## Case study

Read the following extract from a routine visit by an Environmental Health Officer to a fish and chip shop:

The owner was preparing the batter. He had a skin complaint, and his neck and hands were covered in spots and blisters. He took the EHO into the food preparation area. The EHO put on a clean white coat and hat. She washed her hands in a small wash hand basin; soap, paper towels and cold water were available. It was a hot day and the back door was open. Two long ribbons of flypaper hung from the ceiling. An employee wearing a thin plastic apron was taking a delivery of fresh fish and frozen food.

Six large sacks of potatoes lay on the floor and were stacked against the wall. A mop bucket was filled with dirty water. Cleaning products were stored by the potatoes.

The premises had two large stainless-steel sinks. Each was filled with used equipment and utensils.

The EHO entered a large walk-in fridge. A long strip of cardboard had been placed on the floor. Her temperature probe revealed this was operating at the correct temperature of 4°C. Fresh fish was stored on a top shelf uncovered and next to a tray of cooked pies.

Next, the EHO inspected the hot holding area. The temperature dial on the hot holding cabinet was set at 75°C; the EHO's own probe revealed a temperature of 65°C. The cabinet contained a selection of pies, cooked fish and sausages.

### Questions

1   Identify as many food safety and hygiene issues as you can.
2   Write a letter to the manager of the fish and chip shop informing him of your concerns. Give instructions on how to improve food safety and hygiene.

# Practice questions

1   Ronaldo has booked his 21st birthday party at Razzlers' pub. He has paid for 30 guests to have a sit-down buffet.

Suggest **four** ways that Razzlers' pub could meet the needs of Ronaldo and his guests with the equipment the pub could offer and the choice of menu items.

a   Equipment offered.                                                                                                (4 marks)

b   Choice of menu items (do not list individual dishes).                                                            (4 marks)

2   The chef at Razzlers' pub is updating the Hazard Analysis Critical Control Points (HACCP) form before the party. Different hazards are stated in the tables below.

a   Suggest a control point and a reason for each control for the storage of food.                              (4 marks)

| Process | Hazard | Control points | |
|---|---|---|---|
| Storage of food | High-risk food is stored at room temperature | Control | |
| | | Reason | |
| | Hot food is put in the fridge | Control | |
| | | Reason | |

b   Suggest a control point and a reason for each control for the preparation of food.                         (4 marks)

| Process | Hazard | Control points | |
|---|---|---|---|
| Preparation of food | Food may be out of date | Control | |
| | | Reason | |
| | Cross-contamination may occur | Control | |
| | | Reason | |

3   Following the buffet, several guests developed signs of food-induced ill health (food poisoning). List **two** visible and **two** non-visible symptoms.                                         (4 marks)

4   There are several food poisoning bacteria that may have caused ill health to the Razzlers' guests. Name **four** different food poisoning bacteria.                                              (4 marks)

5   Following the outbreak of food poisoning, the EHO was contacted to carry out an investigation.

a   What does EHO stand for?                                                                                       (1 mark)

b   Name **one** other responsibility of an EHO.                                                                   (1 mark)

# Unit 2 Hospitality and catering in action

## ABOUT THIS UNIT

In this unit you will develop and apply your knowledge and understanding of nutrition, and learn how to make nutritious meals.

You will use the knowledge and experience you gained in Unit 1 to help you with Unit 2.

You will learn about:
- the skills needed to prepare, cook and present nutritious dishes
- food safety, and meeting the nutritional needs of different groups of people
- the operation of the front and back of house
- health and safety in hospitality and catering provision
- preventing food-induced ill health
- how to review your work effectively.

## TOPICS

The topics covered in this unit are:
2.1 The importance of nutrition
2.2 Menu planning
2.3 The skills and techniques of preparation, cooking and presentation of dishes
2.4 Evaluating cooking skills

## HOW WILL I BE ASSESSED?

This unit is assessed internally by your teacher, and a sample of work is sent to the exam board to be moderated.

The Unit 2 assessment contributes 60 per cent to the overall qualification. It takes 12 hours and is worth 120 marks.

An assignment brief will be provided by the exam board, which will include a scenario and several tasks.

A new assignment brief will be set every year by the exam board and given to you by your teacher.

# 2.1 The importance of nutrition

**Getting started**

1 Discuss with a partner the names of all of the nutrients you know and what these do in the body (their functions).

2 Make a bullet-point list of these nutrients and their functions.

## 2.1.1 Understanding the importance of nutrition

Nutrition is an important topic in Unit 2. You will need to know what the nutrients do; this is also known as their function. In addition to this, you will need to know why we need to eat a balanced and varied diet. Having a varied diet with lots of different foods is the best way to make sure we consume all of the nutrients we need.

Food provides the nutrients and energy that the body needs for growth, repair and maintenance, so that it can stay healthy and work properly.

There are five main groups of nutrients:

1 protein
2 fat
3 carbohydrate
4 vitamins
5 minerals.

These can be broken up into two groups – macronutrients and micronutrients – as discussed below.

## The macronutrients

The macronutrients are:

■ protein
■ fat
■ carbohydrate.

We will now look at each of these in turn.

# Protein

Protein is needed:

- for the growth of all body cells and tissue (for example for spurts of growth in teenagers)
- for the maintenance and repair of all body tissue (for example as a result of natural wear and tear or injury)
- to provide an energy source if the body doesn't receive enough energy from carbohydrates or fat.

Some groups of people need more protein than others. For example, children and pregnant people need more protein for growth, and everyone needs more protein after injury to repair the body.

Proteins are made up of **amino acids**. There are ten essential amino acids that must come from food. **High biological value proteins**, such as meat, fish, eggs, cheese and soya beans, contain all of the essential amino acids. **Low biological value proteins**, such as beans, peas, lentils, nuts and cereals, are missing one or more of the essential amino acids.

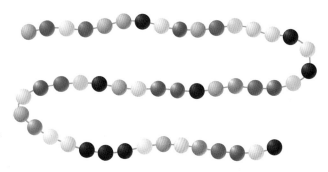

▲ **An amino acid chain**

> ## Key terms
>
> **Amino acid** the basic component of all proteins
>
> **High biological value protein** a protein that contains all of the essential amino acids
>
> **Low biological value protein** a protein that lacks one or more of the essential amino acids

# Fat

Fats are an important source of energy; they also insulate the body. Fats are solid at room temperature whereas oils are liquid. Some fats you can see, such as butter, lard and suet, while others you can't see, such as the fat in cheese or cakes. Animal fats include butter, lard, oily fish, fatty meats, cheese and cream. Oils such as sunflower oil and olive oil, nut and nut products (for example peanut butter) and seeds (for example sesame seeds) are vegetable fats.

▲ **Different types of fats**

## Key terms

**Sugary foods** foods high in sugar, such as jam, cakes, biscuits and ice cream

**Starchy foods** foods high in starch, such as pasta, rice, potatoes and bread

# Carbohydrate

Carbohydrates provide the main source of energy for the body. Carbohydrates are made by plants in a process called photosynthesis. They may come from **sugary foods**, such as cakes, sweets and biscuits, or **starchy foods**, such as bread, rice, pasta and potatoes.

▲ **Potatoes are a starchy carbohydrate**

Table 2.1 **Macronutrients, their main sources and functions**

| Macronutrient | Main food sources | Function |
|---|---|---|
| Protein | Meat, fish, milk, cheese, eggs, beans, soya, cereals, quinoa | Growth, repair and maintenance, and a secondary source of energy |
| Fat | Butter, lard, vegetable oils, cream, nuts, seeds | Energy and insulating the body (warmth) |
| Carbohydrate | Starchy foods such as bread, rice, pasta, potatoes<br><br>Sugary foods such as biscuits, cakes, sweets | Slow-release energy<br><br>Fast-release energy |

## Activity

Make your own information sheet to show the names of the macronutrients, their main food sources and functions. Include images and your choice of some other food sources.

Your teacher may give you a copy of the table on macronutrients for you to add some more information. Add some images of the foods named and to show the functions of each nutrient.

### Extension activity

Add a column to the table and include examples of recipes that are high in each of the macro-nutrients.

# The micronutrients

The micronutrients are vitamins and minerals.

There are lots of different vitamins and minerals. The ones you need to know about are described below.

## Vitamins

### Vitamins A and D

These vitamins are **fat-soluble**, which means they dissolve in fat; they are found in foods such as butter, cheese and whole milk. Vitamin A can come from animal products such as dairy foods, egg yolks and liver, and fruit and vegetables such as carrots, apricots and mangoes.

> **Key term**
>
> **Fat-soluble vitamins** vitamins that dissolve in fat; these are vitamins A and D

▲ **Foods that contain vitamin A**

Vitamin D can be made by the body when the skin is exposed to sunlight, or can be consumed in the diet by eating foods such as oily fish and fat spreads.

▲ **Foods that contain vitamin D**

## Vitamin C and B group vitamins

These vitamins are water-soluble, which means they dissolve in water. The B group vitamins may be found in a wide range of foods, but especially wholegrain cereal foods such as wholemeal bread, seeds and beans. The B group vitamins are also added to white flour by law in the UK, and to many breakfast cereals.

▲ **Foods that contain vitamin C**

▲ **Foods that contain the B group vitamins**

Vitamin C is found in fruits and vegetables (except dried varieties), especially when they are fresh or frozen.

# Minerals

You will need to know about the following minerals:

- calcium
- iron
- magnesium
- potassium
- sodium.

▲ **Foods that contain calcium**

## Calcium

Calcium is found in milk and dairy foods. It is also found in plant-based foods such as broccoli and almonds, and soya products such as tofu, although it is less easily absorbed from these.

## Iron

Iron is found in animal products, such as red meat. It is also found in some plant-based foods, such as green leafy vegetables and cocoa.

▲ **Foods that contain iron**

## Magnesium

Magnesium is present in many foods, especially those that are vegetable in origin; this is because magnesium is found in **chlorophyll**, the green pigment in plants.

▲ **Foods that contain magnesium**

## Potassium

Potassium is present in almost all foods; the main sources are potatoes, vegetables, fruit, bananas and fruit juices.

▲ **Foods that contain potassium**

**▲ Foods that contain sodium**

## Sodium

Sodium is found in salty foods such as cheese, bacon, bread, smoked fish, ready meals and salted nuts.

**Table 2.2 Food sources and functions of micronutrients**

| Micronutrient | Main food sources | Function |
| --- | --- | --- |
| Vitamin A | Eggs, oily fish, liver, whole milk, spinach, carrots, sweet potatoes, mangoes, apricots | Helps sight in poor light and strengthens the **immune system**<br>Needed for healthy skin and mucous membranes |
| Vitamin B group | Bread, eggs, meat, chicken, milk, potatoes | Keeps the skin, eyes and nervous system healthy<br>Needed for the release of energy from food |
| Vitamin C | Fruits and vegetables, especially oranges, blackcurrants, broccoli, strawberries, peppers | Helps the body to absorb iron<br>Keeps body cells healthy and helps the healing process |
| Vitamin D | Whole milk, butter, oily fish, eggs, **fortified cereals**, fat spreads | Helps the body to absorb the mineral calcium |
| Calcium | Nuts, bread, fortified cereals, cheese, milk, green leafy vegetables, oily fish, soya, tofu | Builds strong bones and teeth<br>Controls muscle function and heartbeat<br>Helps with blood clotting |
| Iron | Red meat, cabbage, kale, lentils, tofu, quinoa, egg yolks | Makes the **haemoglobin** in the red blood cells that carry oxygen around the body |
| Magnesium | Nuts, seeds (for example Brazil nuts, sunflower seeds), wholegrain breakfast cereals, wholegrain and seeded breads, brown rice, quinoa | Needed for the release of energy from food<br>Needed for some glands in the body to work normally |
| Potassium | Bananas, broccoli, parsnips, pulses, nuts and seeds, fish, beef, chicken, turkey | Helps to control the balance of fluids in the body<br>Helps the heart muscle to work properly |
| Sodium | Salt, cheese, bacon, bread, smoked fish, ready meals, salted nuts | Essential to balance fluids in the body, such as blood<br>Excess sodium leads to **high blood pressure**, strokes and heart attacks |

## Water

Water is essential for the survival of the human body. It has many functions: it cools the body by sweating, evaporating from the surface of the skin to cool the body down. Water also transports waste products from the body.

Our body fluids, such as blood, urine and sweat, contain a lot of water. Our digestive juices also contain a lot of water, so the essential process of digestion can't occur without a good supply of water. Water helps to prevent **constipation** by softening solid waste.

It is also needed by the kidneys to filter impurities from the blood during the production of urine.

Most people need about two litres of water (or other watery drinks) every day. If insufficient water is consumed, it can lead to dehydration.

Many foods, such as vegetables and fruits, provide water, but we mainly get our water from drinks. In the UK, it is safe to drink tap water and this is the best way to make sure we take in enough liquid to stay healthy. In hot weather and during exercise, we lose more water and so extra is needed. More water is also often needed during illness.

If we don't drink enough water, we feel thirsty and become dehydrated. We may have dark urine or produce less urine, experience a headache or lack of energy, or feel light-headed.

▲ **Drinking tap water is a great way to stay hydrated**

# Dietary fibre

**Dietary fibre** (also known as non-starch polysaccharide, or NSP for short) is a type of carbohydrate. It is found in the cell walls of vegetables, fruits, pulses and cereal grains. Root vegetables such as potatoes (especially with the skin on), carrots, fresh fruit, dried fruit, pulses and nuts are also high in fibre.

More dietary fibre is present in wholegrain cereals, such as wholemeal bread and brown rice.

Dietary fibre is not digested, but passes through the body unchanged. It allows the digestive system to remain healthy and work properly by stimulating the action of the intestines to move food waste through it at a faster pace. If food stays in the digestive system for too long, toxins from food waste can be absorbed into the bloodstream and cause illness.

Diets high in fibre are especially helpful to people with diabetes because the fibre helps to slow down the release of glucose into the bloodstream.

In the UK, most diets are too low in fibre as a consequence of being too low in fruits and vegetables, and lacking in wholegrain cereals. This can lead to constipation. Fibre intake can be increased by eating the recommended five a day of fruit and vegetables, and choosing wholegrain foods in place of processed foods (for example choosing wholemeal bread instead of white bread or brown rice in place of white rice).

> ## Key term
>
> **Dietary fibre** a type of carbohydrate found in the cell walls of vegetables, fruits, pulses and cereal grains; also known as non-starch polysaccharide (NSP)

▲ **Bran flakes are a good source of fibre**

# Knowledge check

1 Name four foods that are a good source of protein.
2 State the two main groups of carbohydrates.
3 Describe two functions of water in the body.
4 Describe two functions of vitamin C in the body.
5 Name three foods that are a good source of potassium.

> **Activity**
>
> 1  Look at the list below. Without looking at any food labels, estimate which of the foods listed contain the most sugar. Indicate which ones you think are in the top five.
>     - Tomato ketchup
>     - Stir-in sweet-and-sour sauce
>     - Salad cream
>     - Low-fat fruit yoghurt
>     - Choc ice
>     - Frosted cornflakes
>     - Regular cola
>     - Baked beans
>     - Fresh fruit juice
>     - Chocolate spread
>     - Fruit pastilles
> 2  From a display of different food products (suggestions above) find out from the labels the sugar content in grams of 100 g of each of the foods. Make a table to show the results.
> 3  Discuss ways in which an adult might reduce the amount of sugar in their daily diet. Make a PowerPoint display of your findings and use this to present them to the class.

# Different life-stages

## Children

### Babies

Babies should have milk for their first six months (ideally breast milk as this is the most natural source of food for human babies and changes to meet babies' nutritional needs as they grow). After six months they can begin to try different foods, starting with vegetables and fruits. They need lots of energy for growth and movement. Salt and sugar should not be added to babies' foods.

Iron and vitamin C are important nutrients for babies as their natural iron stores are low after having milk for six months.

▲ **Babies should not have salt or sugar added to their food**

### Toddlers

Toddlers have **growth spurts** as well as an active lifestyle. As their stomachs are small, they cannot eat large meals; instead they need to eat regular smaller meals as well as snacks and drinks throughout the day, to provide sufficient energy and nutrients.

Important nutrients for babies and toddlers are:
- protein for growth and repair
- calcium and vitamin D for strong bones and teeth
- iron and vitamin C for healthy red blood cells
- the B group vitamins, which help the body to release energy from carbohydrates.

> **Key term**
>
> **Growth spurt** a rapid increase in height

## Teenagers

The body goes through many changes when children become teenagers. They, or those preparing food for them, should follow the guidelines of the Eatwell Guide (see section 2.2.1) to ensure a good balance of foods and nutrients. The Eatwell Guide sets out the ideal balance of a healthy diet. This should consist mainly of fruits and vegetables. Starchy carbohydrates, such as bread, rice, pasta and potatoes, should form the next largest part of the diet. Protein foods such as beans, pulses, fish, eggs and meat are also important, but needed in smaller amounts than fruits and vegetables or starchy foods. Dairy and dairy-alternative foods, such as milk, soya drink and low-sugar yoghurts, are important but lower-fat options should be chosen. Finally, oils and spreads should be included, but in much smaller amounts as they are high in energy. However, they are important as they provide essential fats needed for good health.

▲ **Teenagers have growth spurts and need lots of energy from their food**

Like toddlers, teenagers have rapid growth spurts. Their appetites increase and so bigger portions should be provided in most cases, except when they are very inactive.

It is particularly important to include the following nutrients:
- protein for growth and repair
- calcium and vitamin D for strong bones and teeth
- iron and vitamin C for healthy red blood cells; some people need more iron due to **menstruation** (periods).

# Adults

## Early adulthood (age 19 to 44)

Early adulthood begins straight after the teenage years. As adults are no longer growing after the age of about 21, their nutritional needs change, and they need less energy and calcium than teenagers do.

In the UK, early adulthood can be the start of weight gain as less food is needed. Avoiding foods high in fat and sugar will help to prevent weight gain.

Nutrients that are especially important in early adulthood include calcium and vitamin D, as the skeleton is not completely formed until about 30 years of age; this is called 'peak bone mass'.

Iron and vitamin C are also important for healthy red blood cells. Some people will be menstruating and will therefore need extra iron. Vitamin C helps the **absorption** of iron.

> **Key terms**
>
> **Menstruation** when a person has a monthly period
>
> **Absorption** when digested nutrients are absorbed into the bloodstream

▲ **Adults should reduce the amount of fat and sugar in their diet to prevent weight gain**

### Pregnancy

During pregnancy, people require a healthy, balanced diet. Food should be prepared carefully as pregnant people are a vulnerable group and therefore more at risk from food poisoning.

Folic acid is needed at the start of pregnancy to avoid birth defects. Protein is needed to ensure the growth of the baby, calcium and vitamin D are required for the development of the baby's skeleton, and iron and vitamin C for the development of the baby's blood supply. Foods high in vitamin A should be avoided.

During the last three months of pregnancy more energy (calories) is required.

### Middle adulthood (age 45 to 64)

Energy needs often continue to decrease in middle age. People who continue to menstruate (have periods) until the age of about 50 years will need a good supply of iron in their diets.

Foods high in fat and sugar should be avoided to prevent weight gain. Many adults in the UK are overweight or **obese**, which can lead to heart disease and some cancers, in addition to **mobility problems**.

### Late adulthood (age 65 and over)

Older people still need a well-balanced diet containing all the nutrients in the correct proportions, but fewer **calories** (energy) are needed as older bodies tend to slow down and become less efficient than they were. Sugary or fatty foods should be avoided as these contain a lot of energy, which may lead to people becoming overweight or obese.

Again, following the Eatwell Guide (see page 143) is important to ensure the correct balance of the diet. Eating at least five portions of fruits or vegetables per day is helpful to ensure a good supply of vitamins, which can help to prevent heart disease and some cancers. During late adulthood, constipation can become a problem. To treat this, plenty of watery drinks, including tea and squashes, are useful. Extra dietary fibre will also aid digestion. To protect bone health, calcium and vitamin D are also needed. Iron and vitamin C are also important to keep red blood cells healthy and to prevent tiredness caused by anaemia. Iron deficiency anaemia occurs when insufficient iron in the diet causes red blood cells to become unable to carry enough oxygen around the body. This can lead to a pale skin colour and tiredness, both of which are typical symptoms of anaemia.

▲ **During late adulthood portion size should be reduced as less energy is needed**

## Activity

In a team, you will be given one of the target groups above. Plan a presentation to your class using either A3 paper or a PowerPoint slide show to outline the nutritional needs of your target group.

# Special dietary needs

## Lifestyle

Many people have busy lifestyles and this affects their food choices. Some will have long working hours, often travelling longer distances from home. They are likely to have less time for breakfast and will eat on the move. It could also reduce the time and motivation they have to cook meals every evening.

Working parents can find preparing meals after having worked all day tiring and so, for convenience, they may choose to eat outside the home or buy takeaway food, ready meals or convenience foods.

## Occupation

Energy requirements are higher for people with physically active occupations, such as builders, cleaners or sportspeople.

Occupations that are less active are those that are usually carried out while sitting down for most of the day, such as office jobs or driving. This requires a lower energy intake.

Those with less active jobs may need to limit their food intake and might need to count their energy (kcal) intake carefully, to ensure the correct energy balance. Those with more active jobs might need to choose higher-energy meals.

In April 2022, it became compulsory for food businesses with over 250 employees to put calorie information on their menus. If they fail to do this, they can be fined. Smaller food businesses may do this by choice.

If the average female needs 2000 kcal a day, a main meal would need to be in the region of 600 kcal if three meals are eaten a day. For the average male, this would increase to 2500 kcal a day, so each main meal would need to be about 800 kcal. This would allow for additional snacks to be eaten throughout the day.

However, it is common for people with less active occupations to take part in more exercise outside of work hours, and for those with active occupations to have less active hobbies and leisure time.

Given that most working people are at work for about eight hours a day, the type of occupation will have a major impact on the number of kcal needed on a daily basis.

## Age

From birth until old age, nutritional needs change, so this needs to be taken into consideration when planning menus to suit people of different ages. (See pages 126–9 for further information.)

## Activity level

Your body needs energy for every function and movement it performs. For example:

- breathing
- the function of **internal organs**
- digesting food
- activities such as walking, running, cycling, and even sitting down.

Your energy needs change depending on the activities you do, as well as your age, health and gender.

The amount of energy you need to stay alive for 24 hours when warm and resting is known as your **basal metabolic rate (BMR)**.

Your **physical activity level (PAL)** shows your daily activity level as a number. If you are not very active, you will have a lower PAL than someone who is very active.

PAL and BMR can be used to work out how much energy is needed from food in order to maintain your lifestyle:

$$Physical\ activity\ level = \frac{Total\ energy\ expenditure\ over\ 24\ hours}{Basal\ metabolic\ rate\ over\ 24\ hours}$$

## Special diets

Some people follow a special diet for health reasons, for example they want to improve their health by eating less sugar, salt and fat, and by eating more dietary fibre.

Others choose to avoid certain foods in their diets for religious or **ethical** reasons. Vegetarians do not eat meat and vegans do not eat any animal products, for example.

### Key terms

**Internal organs** the organs inside the body, such as the heart, lungs and kidneys

**Basal metabolic rate (BMR)** how many calories you need to stay alive for 24 hours when warm and resting

**Physical activity level (PAL)** the amount of physical activity you do each day, for example sitting, standing, running and exercise

**Ethical** good or morally correct (for example behaviour)

# Medical conditions

The term 'food allergy' describes a serious reaction caused by eating certain foods and may cause life-threatening symptoms. For more on food allergies and the foods that cause them, see section 1.4.1 (pages 84–6).

| | | | |
|---|---|---|---|
| Cereals containing gluten | Peanuts | Nuts | Milk |
| Soya | Mustard | Lupin | Eggs |
| Fish | Crustaceans | Molluscs | Sesame seeds |
| Celery | Sulphur dioxide | | |

▲ **Ingredients that can cause food allergies or reactions**

'Food intolerance' describes when people are sensitive to certain foods and may have difficulty digesting them. Lactose intolerance and gluten intolerance are two examples (see Table 2.3). For more on food intolerances, see section 1.4.1.

Table 2.3 **Food intolerances**

| Food intolerance | Foods that should be avoided |
|---|---|
| Lactose | Lactose is the sugar in milk, so anything with milk in it should be avoided. For example:<br>■ milk<br>■ cheese<br>■ yoghurt<br>■ cream<br>Always check ingredients labels for milk as it is added to many different foods. |
| Gluten | Gluten is a protein found in wheat and other cereals, such as rye and barley. The following foods should be avoided unless you are sure they are gluten-free:<br>■ pasta<br>■ biscuits<br>■ bread<br>■ cakes<br>■ breakfast cereals<br>■ sauces |

## Type 2 diabetes

Type 2 diabetes is the most common type of diabetes in the UK. The condition causes sugar in the blood to reach too high a level. Many people have type 2 diabetes without realising it.

The main symptoms of type 2 diabetes are feeling tired all the time, feeling thirsty and passing more urine than usual.

Some people are more at risk than others of developing type 2 diabetes, especially if they are overweight or obese. Age is also a factor – people aged over 40 are more likely to develop type 2 diabetes. People who eat fatty, salty and sugary foods often are more at risk. People who have high blood pressure and do not exercise regularly put themselves at additional risk of type 2 diabetes.

## Cardiovascular disorder

Cardiovascular disorder covers a group of diseases, including coronary heart disease and stroke. If blood flow is reduced or stopped by a blood clot or narrowing of the blood vessels, damage may be caused to the body. If this happens in the heart, it can cause a **heart attack**; if this happens in the brain, the person will have a stroke.

### *Coronary heart disease*

Coronary heart disease occurs when the blood vessels to the heart become blocked with fatty deposits. This can cause **angina** if the blood flow is restricted, or a heart attack if the blood supply is cut off completely. It is the main cause of death in the UK.

### *Stroke*

A stroke occurs when the blood supply to the brain is cut off. A stroke may cause physical disability, brain injury or even death. It is the third most common cause of death in the UK after heart disease and cancer.

**Key terms**

**Heart attack** when the blood supply to the heart is cut off

**Angina** when the blood supply to the heart is restricted

## 2.1 The importance of nutrition

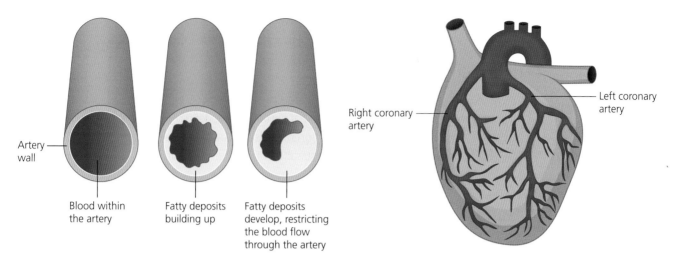

Artery wall

Blood within the artery

Fatty deposits building up

Fatty deposits develop, restricting the blood flow through the artery

Right coronary artery

Left coronary artery

▲ **How fatty deposits build up in the blood vessels**

▲ **If the coronary arteries become blocked with fatty substances this can cause a heart attack**

## Reducing the risk of cardiovascular disease

The following tips will help to prevent cardiovascular disease.

- Follow the Eatwell Guide and do not overeat. Being overweight increases a person's risk of getting heart disease.
- People should not drink too much alcohol – no more than 14 units a week spread over three or more days.
- It's better if parents set a good example. If they eat healthily and take exercise, their children are more likely to do the same.
- A low-fat diet helps to prevent cardiovascular disease. No more than 35 per cent of the total energy in your diet should come from fat.
- By reducing the amount of salt in your diet, you reduce your risk of developing cardiovascular disease.
- Eating too much sugar is a risk factor for cardiovascular disease. You should get about 50 per cent of your energy from carbohydrates, but only 5 per cent of this should come from **free sugars** – these are added sugars such as granulated sugar or honey. Swapping sugary drinks for water or milk, and occasionally sugar-free soft drinks, is a good way of reducing sugar consumption.
- Some breakfast cereals are deceptively high in sugar, so it's a good idea to look at food labels to check the sugar content before buying them.

## Iron deficiency anaemia

Iron deficiency anaemia occurs when there are insufficient red blood cells. Red blood cells transport oxygen around the body; when there are not enough of them, the body becomes short of oxygen.

Anaemia may cause pale skin, breathlessness, **heart palpitations**, tiredness, dizziness or fainting. To find out if you have this type of anaemia, you will need a blood test.

Iron deficiency anaemia may be caused by a lack of iron in the diet. People who have heavy periods (menstruation) are at more of risk of this type of anaemia.

It may be treated with iron tablets or a diet high in iron and vitamin C. Vitamin C helps the body to absorb iron so should be included in dishes and meals containing iron (serving a side salad with meat dishes, for example).

> **Key terms**
>
> **Free sugars** sugars that are added to food (they are not part of the cell wall of a plant)
>
> **Heart palpitation** a noticeably rapid, strong or irregular heartbeat

## Key terms

**Wesak** Buddha's birthday, and one of the most important Buddhist festival, it reminds Buddhists of the importance of the life of Buddha

**Lent** The 40 days and 40 nights before Easter when certain food and drinks are given up

**Kosher** food that is permitted under Jewish dietary laws

**Halal** something that is permitted under Islamic law, for example particular foods and methods of preparing them

**Ramadan** a month in the year when Muslims fast from dawn to sunset

▲ **Sweets used as gifts for Diwali, the festival of lights**

▲ **Apples dipped in honey, celebrating Rosh Hashanah**

If iron deficiency anaemia is left untreated, a person is more likely to get infections as the body needs iron for the normal functioning of the immune system.

# Religious beliefs

People's food choices may be affected by their religious beliefs, which may not allow them to eat certain foods or to eat at certain times. Religious festivals can also involve families and friends eating traditional foods as part of the celebration. Food outlets often create menus with dishes suitable for different religions.

## Buddhists (Buddhism)

There are no set dietary laws in Buddhism, but many Buddhists are vegetarian due to the principle of non-violence. Alcohol is discouraged because of the effects on the mind. Buddhist monks and nuns are usually very strict and often fast in the afternoon. **Wesak**, one of the most important Buddhist festivals, is celebrated with lots of vegetarian dishes as a symbol of the compassion for all living creatures.

## Christians (Christianity)

In the 40 days and 40 nights leading up to Easter, many Christians will observe **Lent** and give up certain food and drink. Some Christians will avoid meat for the whole of Lent, while others might eat fish on Fridays in place of meat. It is also common to give up indulgences such as coffee, sweets and alcohol.

## Hindus (Hinduism)

Beef and beef products are not eaten because the cow is considered to be a sacred animal. However, milk is permitted because no animal is killed during the process. In practice, many Hindus are vegetarian because they follow the principle of *ahimsa* (not harming). The consumption of alcohol is strongly discouraged. Diwali is a major Hindu festival; it is also called the festival of lights and is celebrated by exchanging sweets.

## Jewish people (Judaism)

In Judaism, dairy and meat should not be eaten in the same meal; for example, chicken and milk or beef and cheese cannot be eaten together. Pork is not eaten. Only meat that has been slaughtered in a specific way, known as **kosher**, should be eaten. Seafood must have fins and scales, so eating shellfish is not allowed. There are many major Jewish festivals where specific foods are eaten. During Passover a special meal (*Seder*) is eaten and unleavened bread (*matzoh*) is eaten for the duration of Passover. A traditional Rosh Hashanah (Jewish New Year) dish is apples or bread dipped in honey.

## Muslims (Islam)

Muslims do not eat pork, and only eat meat that is **halal** (slaughtered in a specific way). Only seafood with fins and scales should be eaten. Many Muslims consider shellfish unclean. Alcohol is forbidden. Most Muslims fast during the holy month of **Ramadan**, meaning they don't eat or drink during daylight hours. At the end of Ramadan, a three-day festival called Eid al-Fitr is celebrated, where special food is eaten.

## Rastafarians (Rastafarianism)

Rastafarians eat food which is natural, pure, clean or from the earth, this is called I-tal. They try to avoid food which has been chemically modified or contains artificial additives. Most meat, and especially pork, is avoided. They do eat fish, but will not eat fish more than 30 cm long. Rastafarian diets are high in fruits and vegetables because they are naturally from the earth. Salt is not used to flavour food, and alcohol is generally avoided. They prefer to drink herbal teas and fruit juices.

## Sikhs (Sikhism)

Many Sikhs follow a vegetarian diet, but meat is not forbidden, as long as the animal was not killed in a ritualistic manner (like kosher or halal meat). Alcohol and other intoxicants are prohibited. Worship at the Gurdwara, the Sikh temple, concludes with sharing of the sacred Karah Parshad, a dough made from equal parts butter, sugar and flour.

### Activity

Plan a celebration meal suitable for people that practise one of the above mentioned religions.

Your teacher may give you a template to help you plan a main course, dessert and drink for one of the religions given above. Only choose foods that are acceptable to this religion, but make the meal varied and colourful.

### Extension activity

Plan a three-course meal with drinks for one of the religions given above. Give reasons for your choice for each course.

# Vegetarians

People may choose not to eat meat for a variety of reasons:

- they may not like the idea of eating a dead animal, fish or bird
- they think it is cruel to kill animals for food
- their religion may prohibit them from eating meat
- meat can contain quite a lot of saturated fat and cholesterol, so some people become vegetarian to avoid these, replacing them with plant-based foods such as **pulses**, which are lower in fat but still contain protein and iron
- they may do so for economic reasons, as plant-based foods are often cheaper than meat.

In addition, it is considered wasteful to raise animals when the same land space could grow many more crops.

▲ **This trademark means the food/product is suitable for lacto-ovo vegetarians**

## Lacto-vegetarians

**Lacto-vegetarians** do not eat meat, poultry and fish, or products made from animals, such as lard and gelatine. They do not eat eggs either, although they will eat dairy products such as milk, butter, cream, cheese and yoghurt.

This type of diet is varied and nutritional deficiencies are unlikely. As lacto-vegetarians do not eat eggs, which are a good source of iron, extra care should be taken to ensure an adequate supply of iron, along with vitamin C to aid its absorption.

### Key terms

**Pulses** the collective term for peas, beans and lentils

**Lacto-vegetarians** vegetarians who eat no fish, meat, meat products or eggs, but eat dairy products such as cheese and milk

## Key terms

**Lacto-ovo vegetarians** vegetarians who eat no fish, meat or meat products, but eat eggs and dairy foods

**Pescatarians** people who eat no meat or meat products, but eat eggs, fish and dairy foods

**Vegans** vegans eat a completely plant-based diet, containing no food of animal origin or products containing ingredients derived from animals, so no meat, fish or eggs, and no dairy products

## Lacto-ovo vegetarians

The **lacto-ovo vegetarian** is similar to the lacto-vegetarian, but this type of vegetarian eats eggs as well as dairy products. Most UK vegetarians follow this type of diet.

This diet is varied and nutritional deficiencies are unlikely if a balanced diet is followed. The nutrient that is most likely to be low is iron as it is more difficult for the body to absorb iron from non-meat foods.

## Pescatarians

A **pescatarian** diet is the same as an ovo-lacto vegetarian diet, but with the addition of fish and other seafood. There are many reasons why people choose to give up meat and poultry but still decide to eat fish.

- Some people choose to add fish to a vegetarian diet so they can get the health benefits of a vegetarian diet as well as those of eating fish. Fish is a high biological value protein food that contains healthy fats such as omega-3 oil, which is good for heart health. Oily fish such as salmon, trout and mackerel are good sources of omega-3, as the fish oils are dispersed throughout the flesh of these types of fish.
- Some may choose to eat fish as it has less of an environmental impact than meat production.
- Others may choose to eat fish to add variety to their diet and because they like the varied flavours of different types of seafood. It also offers more variety when eating out if the vegetarian choices on a menu are limited.

## Vegans

The Vegan Society created the word '**vegan**' in 1944. Their definition of veganism is:

> … a philosophy and way of living which seeks to exclude – as far as is possible and practicable – all forms of exploitation of, and cruelty to, animals for food, clothing or any other purpose; and by extension, promotes the development and use of animal-free alternatives for the benefit of animals, humans and the environment. In dietary terms it denotes the practice of dispensing with all products derived wholly or partly from animals.

A vegan diet does not contain any animal products, and all foods are plant based, meaning that no meat, eggs or dairy foods are eaten. When following a vegan diet, it is important to plan meals correctly, so that they supply all the essential nutrients. Vegan foods need to be selected to make sure they contain enough protein, calcium and vitamin D, iron and vitamin C, vitamin A and some B group vitamins, which could be lacking in a vegan diet.

The protein foods in a vegan diet are mainly low biological value. This means that one or more of the essential amino acids are missing. Low biological value protein foods need to be combined to produce complete proteins to make sure all of the amino acids are provided. For example, lentil soup and bread demonstrate protein complementation as the amino

▲ **This trademark is owned by the Vegan Society, a registered charity, to help consumers easily identify a vegan product**

acid lacking in the bread is present in the lentils, and the amino acid lacking in the lentils is present in the bread. By combining foods, vegans can make sure they get all of the essential amino acids they need in each meal. In this way vegans can make sure they get all the essential amino acids by eating different low biological value protein foods together.

## Knowledge check

1 Explain which nutrients are especially important for babies.
2 Explain why toddlers should be given smaller portion sizes.
3 Why should adults avoid eating foods that are high in fat and sugar regularly?
4 What is PAL? How is it calculated?
5 State two foods that could cause intolerance.
6 List two nutrients that could treat iron deficiency anaemia.
7 Name a religious festival and the types of foods eaten at this festival.
8 Explain the health benefits of a pescatarian diet.

## 2.1.2 How cooking methods can impact on nutritional value

Different cooking methods can have an impact on the nutritional value of food.

In this section, we are going to look at nine different cooking methods and how each of these can change the nutritional value of food. Some cooking methods cause a gain in nutrients – for instance, frying food increases the fat content. Other cooking methods cause nutrients to be lost – for example, grilling causes the loss of some water-soluble vitamins, such as B group vitamins and vitamin C.

## The impacts of different cooking methods on nutritional value

For healthy eating, we should select cooking methods that retain as many vitamins and minerals as possible, and we should take care not to increase the fat content of food too much. Cooking methods that are quick and either avoid or limit the use of fat and intense heat, such as steaming and stir-frying, are good choices. Other cooking methods that use intense heat with prolonged cooking times, such as baking, cause the most nutrient loss.

Table 2.4 **Different cooking methods and their impacts on nutritional value**

| Method | Impacts | Visual example |
|---|---|---|
| **Baking** | This does not affect the minerals calcium and iron. Vitamin C and B group vitamins are lost due to the heat and often long cooking times inside the oven. Some foods can be baked in their skins and so retain dietary fibre (for example, potatoes and butternut squash). No extra fat is added during baking. | |
| **Boiling** | Vitamin C, vitamins from the B group, iron and calcium will leach (seep out) into the cooking water. However, boiling is a relatively quick method of cooking so the loss of nutrients is not too great. | |
| **Deep fat frying** | This is a very quick method of cooking, so most vitamins and minerals are not lost. The fat content will greatly increase, however, as the food is completely immersed in oil. | |

| Shallow-frying | Most vitamins and minerals are retained. It is a quick method of cooking. The fat content will increase as fat is absorbed into the food. | |
|---|---|---|
| Stir-frying | Quick, so most vitamins are not usually lost. Only a small amount of oil is used so it is healthy too, in line with the Eatwell Guide. For effective stir-frying, the oil should be heated in the pan or wok until it is very hot before the food is added, so that the food doesn't absorb the oil during the cooking process. | |
| Grilling | Iron and calcium will be retained. Some vitamin C and B group vitamins will be lost due to the intense heat. Fat-soluble vitamins are lost when the fat melts because they will run out of the food. Fat drains off the food so this reduces its fat content, making it healthier. | |
| Poaching | Vitamin C and B group vitamins, iron and calcium will leach into the cooking water. | |
| Roasting | Does not affect calcium and iron. Some vitamin C and B group vitamins are lost due to the heat. This loss can be large due to the long cooking times involved in roasting. | |
| Steaming | There is no contact with the water during steaming so vitamin C and B group vitamins, iron and calcium will not leach into the cooking water. There is some loss of the water-soluble vitamins due to the high heat of the steam, but cooking times are shorter. | |

# Knowledge check

1  Explain why the cooking methods of steaming and stir-frying retain important nutrients.

2  How is the nutritional value of food affected by deep-frying?

## Activity

1 Find out more about proteins and how low biological value protein foods can be combined to produce high biological value dishes and meals.
2 Search the Vegan Society website for ideas and recipes: www.vegansociety.com/resources/nutrition-and-health
3 Find out about bone health and vegan diets, and which foods contribute to strong bones and teeth.
4 Plan a vegan recipe high in iron and calcium to cook in your next practical lesson.

Make a list of ten low biological value protein foods (plant-based foods). Match some of these together to plan three different meals or snacks (for example beans on toast).

### Extension activity

Write an interview with eight to ten questions to ask a vegan, asking about their reasons for following this diet. Include questions on their favourite foods and meal choices.

## Case study

Doctors and nutritionists are worried about teenagers' low intake of minerals.

Many teenagers are not getting enough iron. About 20 per cent of teenage girls are anaemic, a condition caused by a lack of the mineral iron, which can affect both concentration and mood.

Teenagers can be fussy eaters, eating a limited number of foods, and often skip breakfast, which would naturally be higher in minerals if it included yoghurt, eggs and fortified cereals. Instead they eat their calories later in the day, and this tends to be in foods such as chips, fizzy drinks and burgers, which are less nutritious than breakfast foods.

### Questions

1 Find out why teenage girls are more likely to be anaemic than teenage boys.
2 Which vitamin helps the absorption of iron?
3 Why is skipping breakfast a bad habit for teenagers?
4 Suggest an easy-to-eat and nutritious breakfast for teenagers that is high in iron and vitamin C.
5 What advice would you give to teenagers about the importance of vitamins and minerals?

# 2.2 Menu planning

## What will I learn?
In this topic you will gain knowledge and understanding of the following areas:
2.2.1 Factors affecting menu planning
2.2.2 How to plan production

## Getting started
Using bullet points, list all the things you can think of that a chef would need to consider when making a menu plan for the day in a busy restaurant. For example:
- How many customers will need to be served?

## 2.2.1 Factors affecting menu planning

You will need to think about the following things when planning menus.

## Cost

Food costs form a large percentage of the total costs of catering establishments. It is therefore essential that dishes are costed accurately. Food costs need to be controlled so that the catering establishment makes a **profit** and stays in business. When buying food, it is important to order the correct amount of the highest-quality food at the best price. It is also important to monitor stock to make sure it is rotated, so that the oldest food is used up first, which reduces waste. (See page 107 on stock rotation.)

Recipes should be followed so that the exact amount of ingredients needed are bought and used. Weighing and measuring are crucial too. For example, when cooking pasta or rice, it is easy to overestimate the amounts needed, so by accurately weighing these foods the portion size can be controlled and food waste reduced.

It is important to know how much a recipe is going to cost to make when preparing and cooking food.

The pricing of menu items should be what customers expect and are willing to pay for each dish or meal. Different food services offer food at a wide range of prices to meet the needs of different customers.

If a new restaurant is planning to move into an area, its managers will need to find out about the existing competition to see what is already available and the range of prices that are being charged. It may be that there is a **gap in the market** for a restaurant with a different price range – for example, a high-priced, fine dining option in an area that currently offers only low- to mid-price menus.

Most customers like to have good value for money and to know that they are getting a good deal. Restaurants may offer incentives for customers to visit again, such as a

## Key terms
**Profit** the amount of money remaining when costs have been deducted

**Gap in the market** an unmet consumer demand

loyalty scheme to encourage customers to return, or a money-off voucher for a return visit within a specified time.

# Portion control

Portion control means controlling the amount of food served to each customer. A customer should receive a fair portion for a fair price.

The amount of food in a portion depends on four factors.

1 **Type of customer:** Customers' or clients' needs will vary according to their age, gender, physical activity level (PAL) and their own personal circumstances. For example, a customer may be trying to lose weight or increase muscle bulk.

2 **Type of establishment:** The type of establishment can vary greatly. For example, in the case of a roast dinner, the portion size of the meat will vary depending on whether it is served in a care home or as part of a carvery meal in a restaurant; by contrast, a top-quality restaurant serving a three-course meal would serve a smaller portion size of meat due to the amount of other food that is eaten at the same sitting.

3 **The quality of the food:** Better-quality food often produces a greater number of portions. For example, top-quality fresh strawberries just need to be washed and have their stalks removed (known as dehulling) before serving, with very little waste. Lower-quality strawberries, however, will need to be picked and trimmed to remove any softer parts of the fruit before serving. The time and labour this involves also costs money for the establishment. The flavour and texture of the higher-quality strawberries will also be better and, as a result, will increase customer satisfaction.

4 **The buying price of the food:** The higher the price paid for a food, the higher the quality of that food should be. As stated above, the higher the quality of the food, the greater the number of portions that should be achieved. If lower-quality food has been purchased, it will be difficult to achieve the number of portions necessary to make the required profit. It is possible to buy cuts of fish and meat that are already portioned, without the need for further preparation. Although these usually cost more, they save on preparation time, which will in turn save money.

▲ **Serving ice cream with a scoop achieves the same portion size every time**

# Balanced diets and current nutritional advice

The provision of balanced diets and following current nutritional advice are becoming increasingly important to customers (see pages 126–9 for the nutritional needs of specific groups). Eating out is a regular event for many families, rather than being confined to special occasions, so healthy eating is a priority. The Eatwell Guide presents the government recommendations for a healthy, balanced diet. It is recommended for use with all ages from two upwards.

Nutritional needs change from birth to old age, so the age range of customers should be taken into account when planning a meal to suit them.

▲ **Using fresh strawberries of top quality will avoid food waste**

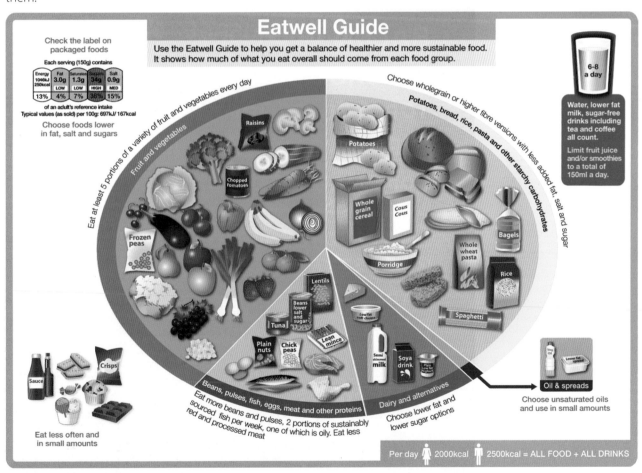

▲ **The Eatwell Guide**

# Time of day

Customers eat out at different times of the day and businesses therefore produce different menus for different meal occasions. It is increasingly common for businesses to be open all day and to offer breakfast menus, morning coffee, lunch, afternoon tea, dinner and supper menus. By providing a round-the-clock menu, an establishment can make full use of its facilities and maximise its profits.

▲ **Eating out at breakfast time is becoming more popular**

# The customers (clients)

A business' customers, sometimes referred to as its client base, will depend on the area and the type of catering establishment – its standards, its size and who it is targeting. Customers need dishes and meals that are varied and include a range of colours, flavours, textures and temperatures. Increasingly customers want to know the nutritional value of food, particularly its fat, sugar and salt content, as well as its energy (calorie, kcal) content, for health reasons. A catering establishment will need to consider who its customers are and put dishes on the menu that meet their needs. Some catering establishments will highlight or code healthy choices on a menu, to guide customers towards healthy, balanced menu choices. This makes it easier for customers with limited nutritional knowledge to make healthier choices.

There should be options for those on special diets, such as gluten-free, vegetarian and vegan. In addition, there should be dishes suitable for people following different religions, such as kosher or halal food for customers who are Jewish or Muslim.

# Equipment available

A large range of equipment is required to produce a menu. This includes hand-held equipment, electrical equipment and specialist equipment. When choosing equipment a catering business will need to consider how much food is to be produced. For instance, if it is catering for large numbers, then larger pans will be needed.

Hand-held equipment includes items such as knives, baking trays, tins, bowls, colanders, sieves, rolling pins, scales, whisks, and various spoons, forks, knives, peelers and saucepans. These come in different sizes and shapes for different uses and help in the production of quality foods.

Electrical equipment includes blenders, food processors, mixing machines, deep fat fryers and cookers. Powered equipment can save time, for example food processors can grate, mix, blend and chop very quickly compared to carrying out these tasks by hand.

Specialist equipment may be used depending on the type of catering establishment, for example specialist coffee grinders and machines in cafés. In pizzerias there may be specialist ovens and tools for cutting pizza. Other specialist equipment might include catering food mixers, meat slicers, sous-vide machines, specialist blenders, pasta machines, waffle and crêpe makers, and ice cream makers.

# Skills of the chef

A chef will need excellent cookery skills, food safety knowledge, leadership and management skills. As well as this, the chef will need **budgeting skills**, the ability to work under pressure (often in a limited space), to meet deadlines and to keep calm in stressful situations.

Chefs need precise practical skills, such as the ability to weigh and measure ingredients for recipes that require accurate and consistent amounts. Chefs also need to take

> **Key term**
>
> **Budgeting skills** managing money by prioritising essential spending before optional spending

into account the needs of individual customers, especially if they have special dietary requirements, such as a food allergy. The chef must ensure that there is no allergen contamination of dishes for such customers.

In addition, a chef needs to be creative in terms of choosing which dishes to cook, and how to construct a menu that is balanced and offers variety to meet the needs of all customers. Such a menu might include a meat dish, a fish dish, and dishes suitable for vegetarians and vegans. Increasingly menus also offer items such as halal meat, to meet the needs of customers who are Muslim.

Different types of chefs specialise in different areas of food preparation, cooking and presentation. For example, pastry chefs make bread, pastries, cakes, **confectionery**, decorated cakes, batters, desserts and other baked goods. They may also be in charge of the dessert menu.

Presenting food attractively for serving is always an important consideration, as is the type of serving dish used. For example, food such as fruit slices or slices of meat can be overlapped, which stops the food looking flat and dull on the plate; if laying out canapés, these could be arranged in contrasting rows, as this will make them look more attractive.

## Time available

If there is a short amount of time available to cook, serve and eat the food, then the range of food offered on the menu will need to be limited.

Fast-food outlets have a smaller menu, using components that can be pre-prepared, so they can cook and serve food quickly.

It is essential that time is managed appropriately by the chef and their team to ensure the waiting time for customers is acceptable and that the time waiting between courses is appropriate for the venue.

To help with time management, many **components of dishes** can be prepared in advance, for example the chopping of vegetables. Some dishes can be made in advance and reheated or baked later, for example soups, cottage pie, lasagne. Many cold desserts can be pre-made so that they are ready to serve.

When customers order a meal, it is likely that more than one dish at a time will need to be prepared so they can be served together. This will require a time plan to ensure that all dishes are ready to be served at the same time. When a meal order comes in, the chef will need to decide which dish needs to be started first. For example, if a cold chicken salad and a vegetable curry with rice are ordered, the chef may put the rice on to boil first; next they may prepare the cold chicken salad and then reheat the curry just before serving, to ensure the two meals are ready to be served together, properly cooked and at the correct temperatures.

## Environmental issues

Food production has a huge impact on the environment. Some types of food production have more of an effect than others. For example, rearing animals for food produces far more **greenhouse gases** than growing plant-based protein foods such as beans.

---

### Key terms

**Confectionery** sweets and chocolate

**Components of dishes** ingredients already combined together; they can be purchased like this (for example ready-made pastry) or to be partly prepared by the chef (for example washed and drained salad ready for use)

**Greenhouse gases** the gases that trap heat and raise the Earth's temperature (for example carbon dioxide, methane, nitrous oxide)

---

The environment includes the air, water and land on which people, animals and plants live. To protect our environment we need to take the following steps.

# Use less energy

There are a number of ways to reduce the amount of energy used. For example:

- adding plant-based foods to menus to replace some animal products
- choosing faster cooking methods, such as stir-frying rather than baking vegetables
- not preheating the oven unless this is crucial for the success of the recipe
- using the oven to cook more than one dish at a time, to make sure the oven is full and all the heat is being used
- matching the size of a saucepan to the size of the hob, to ensure no heat is wasted
- if using gas, making sure the flames are underneath the pan rather than coming up its sides.

# Avoid waste

This can be achieved by ensuring portion sizes are suitable for customers, by practising efficient stock rotation and by ordering the correct amounts of perishable foods, which can be consumed while they are still fresh.

# Reduce water consumption

Water consumption can be reduced by choosing plant proteins in place of animal proteins – for example, cows reared for beef live for about two years and drink about 50 litres of water a day each! Cooking methods that require less water (for example steaming instead of boiling) can be chosen, as can appliances such as dishwashers, which have lower water consumption.

Foods that are produced under conditions that save electricity and water are more sustainable.

# Recycle and reuse

Recycling and reusing should be practised as much as possible (see Table 2.5).

Table 2.5 **Ways to reduce, reuse and recycle**

| Reduce | Cut down on the amount of packaging on food |
|---|---|
| | Conserve energy and water when cooking |
| | Reduce the use of processed foods, which require a lot of energy to manufacture |
| | Use more plant-based foods than animal products; this can hugely reduce water consumption as animals need large amounts of water throughout their lives before slaughter, for drinking and cleaning |
| Reuse | Reuse packaging such as jars, plastic containers and plastic bags where possible, rather than throwing them away |
| | Use leftover food to create another dish. For example:<br>■ use leftover cake to make a trifle<br>■ use leftover meat in a shepherd's pie<br>■ use leftover chicken to make a curry<br>■ use leftover potato in fishcakes or frittata |
| Recycle | Clean, dry food packaging can usually be recycled (for example glass, metal, card, paper, some plastics) |

## Create a sustainable environment

A sustainable environment is one where the demands placed on it can be met without reducing its ability to allow all people to live well, now and in the future.

Sustainable food and farming:
- uses as few resources as possible, and uses renewable energy where possible
- has high standards of animal welfare
- produces healthy and safe food.

The benefits of sustainable food include:
- food establishments building up good relationships with local food producers
- food miles are decreased, therefore reducing the carbon footprint
- animals have less distance to travel, which in turn improves their welfare
- less artificial fertilisers and pesticides are used on the soil, improving the soil quality and protecting wildlife.

A move towards natural food production is thought to be more sustainable. Organic foods have become more popular in recent years as organic methods of food production are more sustainable and less damaging to the environment.

## Time of year

Some foods are seasonal, which means they are available only at certain times of the year. Many fruits and vegetables grown in the UK are seasonal. Developments in transport, and in the preservation and storage of foods, mean that we can import foods from other countries that are not in season in the UK, as well as foods that cannot be grown in the UK. This means that much of our food is available all year round.

However, choosing seasonal foods has many advantages. The foods are more likely to be local, or at least grown in the UK, so the **food miles** will be lower and buying them supports local farms.

In the UK our food travels by boat, aeroplane, lorry and car. Food transport is responsible for adding carbon dioxide into the atmosphere each year. This has an impact on global warming, which is affecting our environment.

Today, food travels much further than it used to because of our demand for:
- seasonal food all year round, for example it is now possible to buy strawberries throughout the year in the UK
- cheap food
- processed food
- a wider range of ingredients from different international cuisines and cultures, which are not produced or grown in the UK.

Some events are planned according to the season, for example outdoor events such as barbecues and picnics may be held in the summer. In the winter, at Christmas time, meal planning may focus on a traditional Christmas dinner, including roast turkey with roast potatoes and vegetables.

The time of year also affects the type of food that is on the menu. Customers may prefer to eat hot food such as soup or curry on a cold day, and a cool salad or ice cream on a hot day, for example.

### Key term

**Food miles** the distance that food is transported as it travels from producer to consumer

# Organoleptic qualities

When we eat food, we use our five senses: sight, smell, touch, taste and hearing. These senses together enable us to assess whether the food we are eating is enjoyable.

The word **organoleptic** refers to the qualities of food that people experience with their senses. This is also known as sensory analysis or sensory evaluation. Eating food should be an enjoyable experience. When planning a menu, dishes that people find **appetising** and that appeal to their senses should be selected.

**Key terms**

**Organoleptic** involving the use of the sense organs, for example to assess the qualities of food

**Appetising** appealing to the senses

▲ **When planning dishes, select foods that appeal to the senses**

# Knowledge check

1 Explain why it is important that all menu items are costed and their selling price calculated before putting a menu together.

2 Outline three different factors a restaurant might consider before deciding on portion sizes for its customers.

3 Consider reasons why many customers are now demanding healthier menu items when eating out.

4 Discuss three reasons why an increasing number of people in the UK are choosing to eat out at breakfast time.

5 Identify three ways in which a business may choose to protect the environment when planning menus and serving food to customers.

6 State two advantages of putting seasonal foods on a menu.

7 Describe the term organoleptic.

## Activity

1 Find out more about reduce, reuse, recycle. Search the website www.lovefoodhatewaste.com for ideas on how to reduce food waste.

2 Make a list of ten tips for reducing food waste.

3 Find out about reducing food waste. Give tips for storing food correctly in the fridge, freezer or cupboards. Include information on the correct storage temperatures.

4 Use this link to find out about date marks on food: www.lovefoodhatewaste.com/about-date-labels

5 Explain the difference between 'use by' dates and 'best before' dates.

6 Using leftover cooked chicken or beans and slightly soft fruit from the fruit bowl (such as apples or bananas), plan a two-course dinner for a family with young children. Your teacher may give you a template to plan a meal using leftover food. The main course will include a leftover protein food such as chicken or beans; the dessert will include very ripe fruit.

### Extension activity

Include recipes and methods for both dishes chosen for question 6 above, clearly indicating which ingredient is in which recipe.

## Case study

A new chef has taken over the kitchen at a secondary school and wants to make varied and interesting lunches for all students and staff.

Previously, meals were unappetising and most students chose to bring in a packed lunch each day.

The new chef has been asked to make appetising and low-cost meals that appeal to everyone and which should include a vegetarian option each day.

### Question

Copy out the table below and, following the example given for Monday, plan one dish for each day of the school's lunch menu for a week. Give reasons for your choice of dishes.

| Day | Main course | Vegetarian option | Dessert | Reasons for choice |
|-----|-------------|-------------------|---------|---------------------|
| Monday | Mild chicken and vegetable curry with steamed rice and naan bread | Mild vegetable and butterbean curry with steamed rice and naan bread | Chocolate and orange mousse with fresh orange slices | Colour: Colourful vegetables can be used in the curry; the dessert has a range of bright colours<br><br>Flavour: A mild spicy flavour<br><br>Texture: A wide range of textures from the bread, rice and softer curry<br><br>Nutrition: Both main courses are high in protein; the dessert provides vitamin C in the oranges and iron in the chocolate |
| Tuesday | | | | Colour:<br>Flavour:<br>Texture:<br>Nutrition: |
| Wednesday | | | | Colour:<br>Flavour:<br>Texture:<br>Nutrition: |
| Thursday | | | | Colour:<br>Flavour:<br>Texture:<br>Nutrition: |
| Friday | | | | Colour:<br>Flavour:<br>Texture:<br>Nutrition: |

## 2.2.2 How to plan production

The dishes on a menu are the starting point for planning how and when they will be produced. This requires careful organisation. After the menu items have been chosen, the order of work and the times when everything should happen should be planned so that the food is prepared, cooked and served on time, while ensuring it is presented well and is safe to eat.

## Commodity list with quantities

The **commodities** that make up recipes need to be ordered in advance. The correct amount of ingredients for each recipe will need to be carefully estimated to provide the correct portion sizes for customers. Normally, a chef would follow a recipe that states the number of people it serves; however, as a basic rule the more people you are catering for, the less food per head you need to provide. For example, for stewing steak, about 225 g per person would be needed for four people, but 170 g per head would be enough for 60 people.

## Example guide to catering quantities

- Meat: roast meat 200 g per person
- Fish: fillets 170 g per person
- Fruit: 110 g per person
- Vegetables: 100 g per person of each vegetable (up to three)
- Dairy foods: 85 g of cheese per person (served after a meal)

## Contingencies

A **contingency** is a backup plan that you can put into place if things go wrong, for example having some spare ingredients in case a recipe goes wrong and you need to start again with new ingredients. You should consider contingencies as part of your production planning.

## Equipment list

Many different types of equipment are used in a catering kitchen. You need to think about all of the equipment you need to produce your dishes, including:
- large equipment (for example ovens and blast chillers)
- small equipment (for example knives, mixing bowls, chopping boards)
- mechanical equipment (for example food mixers and ice cream machines)
- safety equipment (for example first aid kit, fire extinguishers).

## Health, safety and hygiene

Staff need to be trained to store food correctly, and to use equipment in a safe and hygienic way to ensure that the food served is safe to eat.

Staff training is needed so that staff can give accurate information on allergens to customers.

Consideration should be given to the health, safety and hygiene aspects of all stages in the preparation, cooking and serving of dishes.

# Quality points

Each commodity has quality points that should be checked before it is used in a recipe. For example:

- Fresh meat should have a pleasant odour and the colour of the meat should be correct (for example pale pink for pork, pinkish red for lamb and deep red for beef). The fat should be firm and not oily. There should be little or no juices running from the meat.
- Fresh fish should smell fresh (like the sea). Their eyes should be clear and bright, and not sunken.
- Fresh fruit and vegetables should be unbruised and their skin should be undamaged. Fruits such as melons and oranges should feel heavy for their size. Avoid fruits or vegetables with any signs of wilting or mould.
- Eggs should not be broken or cracked. Look for eggs with the British Lion mark as this shows they have been produced in the UK to a high standard and that the hens that laid them have been vaccinated against the bacteria *Salmonella*. As illustrated in the image, the code stamped on an egg covers the entire production chain, meaning that the egg is fully traceable. This allows it to be safely eaten raw if desired (for example in mayonnaise) by all groups of the population.

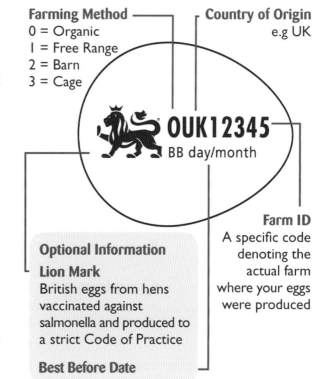

**Farming Method**
0 = Organic
1 = Free Range
2 = Barn
3 = Cage

**Country of Origin**
e.g UK

OUK12345
BB day/month

**Farm ID**
A specific code denoting the actual farm where your eggs were produced

**Optional Information**
**Lion Mark**
British eggs from hens vaccinated against salmonella and produced to a strict Code of Practice

**Best Before Date**

▲ **The British Lion mark explained**

# Sequencing/dovetailing

The order in which the different dishes on the menu are produced is known as **sequencing**; it is also known as **dovetailing**. Correct sequencing will ensure that the quality of dishes matches customer expectations.

Sequencing will include:

- the times when tasks need to be started and finished
- the staff needed to perform different tasks
- the equipment needed at each stage
- details of which dishes need to be prepared first – some foods, such as chicken and tofu, may need to be marinated the night before, while others, such as stir-fry vegetables, can be prepared earlier in the day but not fried until just before serving, so that the vegetables retain their texture, flavour and colour.

**Key terms**

**Sequencing** preparing and cooking dishes in a suitable order so that they are ready to serve on time

**Dovetailing** preparing part of one dish and then part of another dish before the first dish is finished

# Timing

Good timing is very important when preparing meals for customers, so that the food is cooked properly and meals are prepared and served in a reasonable time. In addition, the items comprising each course should be served together at each table.

The time taken for preparation tasks, such as peeling carrots, scrubbing potatoes, filleting fish, freezing ice cream or cooling pastry before filling and decorating, should be known or carefully estimated. Timings allow for the planning of each stage of a recipe, and help in the organisation of which staff and equipment are needed at each stage of preparation, cooking and serving.

# Mise en place

**Key term**

**Mise en place** the preparation of dishes and ingredients before starting to cook

**Mise en place** means preparation before the cooking starts. For example:
- organising equipment and ingredients before beginning to prepare and cook food
- reading and understanding each stage of a recipe
- preparing food carefully to avoid wastage.

# Cooking

Planning should take place before food is cooked to make sure the correct cooking times and temperatures are achieved for all recipes.

Cooking food correctly is essential to make sure it is of high quality, safe to eat and enjoyed by the customers. Cooking food correctly also helps a food business to make a profit, be successful and reduce food waste.

It is very important to make sure that food is cooked according to food safety and hygiene regulations. All risk assessments should be followed to make sure food is cooked according to the plan and is therefore safe to eat.

# Cooling

It is important that food is cooled quickly to make sure that it is not in the temperature danger zone for too long. It should be cooled to below 8°C to meet legal standards (or preferably below 5°C) within 90 minutes to prevent bacteria from multiplying too quickly.

# Hot holding

Hot holding means keeping food at the correct temperature before it is served to customers. The law states that food should be kept at 63°C or higher to ensure its quality and safety before it is served to customers.

# Serving

Orders should be completed and served together so that everyone sitting at a particular table can eat at the same time.

Food should be served hygienically, for example by using tongs or silver service. Waiting staff should avoid touching food with their bare hands.

# Storage

Storage is needed both for ingredients and for the equipment, tools and materials used in a catering kitchen.

Food storage temperatures need to be checked to make sure they are correct:
- food in the fridge should be stored between 0°C and below 5°C (8°C is the legal maximum)
- a freezer should be −18°C or below
- room temperature (for example in cupboards) means between 17°C and 20°C.

For more information on food storage see pages 106–7.

All food storage areas should be kept clean and tidy at all times and a 'clean as you go' policy is the best way to keep on top of this. In addition, scheduled cleaning should take place daily or weekly to make sure all areas are safe and clean.

Storage cupboards for equipment should be emptied and cleaned out once a week as part of a scheduled cleaning routine.

# Drawing up a production plan

When you have considered all of the above points, you will be ready to make your production plan (like the sample in Table 2.6). To do this, you will need:
- a list of ingredients and methods for each recipe
- a list of all the equipment needed for each stage of the recipe
- step-by-step instructions for the preparation, making and presentation of dishes
- correct timings.

**Table 2.6 A sample production plan for Bolognese sauce (green) and cheesecake (red)**

| Time | Activity | Special points |
|---|---|---|
| **Step 1**<br>10 minutes<br>9.00–9.10 | Mise en place<br>Wash hands, put apron on, clean table with antibacterial spray<br>Collect equipment and tools for making cheesecake and Bolognese sauce<br>Weigh and measure ingredients<br>Wash vegetables | Use antibacterial hand wash and spray for the table to ensure that all bacteria are killed<br>Keep high-risk foods, such as cream and meat, separate in the fridge until needed<br>Ensure correct quantities of commodities are used<br>**Contingency:** Have extra commodities in case of recipe failure |
| **Step 2**<br>10 minutes<br>9.10–9.20 | Crush biscuits, melt margarine in a saucepan, add crushed biscuits<br>Place in cheesecake dish, press crumbs down firmly and chill<br>Slice strawberries | Make sure the pan handle is turned to the side to avoid an accident if the pan is knocked |
| **Step 3**<br>10 minutes<br>9.20–9.30 | Make the cheesecake filling by whisking together the cream cheese, icing sugar and double cream<br>Place a little of the filling in a piping bag<br>Spread the filling on the biscuit base and chill this again | Cream cheese and cream are high-risk foods – take them out of the fridge and use immediately<br>**Storage:** Store the cheesecake in the fridge once it has been made<br>Scrape all of the mixture out of the bowl to prevent food waste |
| **Step 4**<br>15 minutes<br>9.30–9.45 | Wash up, dry up and put all the equipment away | Use very hot water and washing-up liquid to ensure all the equipment is clean |
| **Step 5**<br>10 minutes<br>9.45–9.55 | Chop all the vegetables for the Bolognese sauce | Use a brown chopping board, and remember to always cut down towards the chopping board |
| **Step 6**<br>10 minutes<br>9.55–10.05 | Place minced beef in a large saucepan<br>Cook until the meat is browned then add the chopped vegetables, tin of tomatoes, 50 ml water, herbs and tomato purée<br>Bring to the boil and then turn down to simmer for 20 minutes on a low heat | Make sure the pan handle is turned to the side to avoid an accident if the pan is knocked<br>Put a lid on the saucepan, unless the sauce is too runny<br>Check sauce is boiling to ensure bacteria are destroyed |
| **Step 7**<br>15 minutes<br>10.05–10.20 | Wash up, dry up and put all the equipment away<br>Stir the meat sauce regularly | Check area is clean and everything stored in the correct place |
| **Step 8**<br>10 minutes<br>10.20–10.30 | Take cheesecake out of the fridge, decorate with piped filling and sliced strawberries<br>Return to fridge until ready to display | **Completion:** Quality-check the cheesecake – is the piping consistent, are the strawberries cut evenly? |
| **Step 9**<br>15 minutes<br>10.30–10.45 | After 20 minutes of simmering, check flavour and then place Bolognese sauce in container<br>Wash up the frying pan<br>Make sure all work surfaces and sinks are wiped down and clean | **Completion:** Quality-check the sauce – taste it using a clean teaspoon, and add herbs and seasoning as required<br>**Contingency:** Have a selection of serving dishes available, and choose the best one to match the size and colours of dishes once recipe is made |
| **Step 10**<br>10 minutes<br>10.45–10.55 | Garnish the Bolognese sauce, then display the sauce and cheesecake together | **Storage:** Refrigerate the cheesecake and sauce when it has cooled down to room temperature |

## Knowledge check

1 Explain why correct sequencing of the production of dishes is so important.
2 State three important pieces of information that need to be included on a production plan.
3 Name three dishes that would need to be prepared at the start of the production plan and explain why this timing is needed.
4 Name three dishes that need to be cooked just before serving and explain why.
5 Describe what a contingency plan is. Give four examples of what may be included in a contingency plan when making a traditional Christmas meal for 12 people.

## Activity

1 Choose two recipes for dishes that you can make in your next practical lesson.
2 Photocopy these and cut out the various stages of each recipe to sequence (dovetail) the methods.
3 Once you are happy with the order, estimate timings for each stage of the recipes.

## Case study

McDonald's is one of the most popular fast-food chains, with restaurants all over the world. It can be found in more than 100 countries and has about 40,000 restaurants. It is one of the biggest fast-food chains, serving nearly 70 million people every day. Most McDonald's restaurants offer both counter service and a drive-through service. McDonald's mainly sells cheeseburgers, hamburgers, French fries, chicken products, ice cream desserts and soft drinks.

It follows a 'just in time' (JIT) system. JIT is the system of supplying products to customers once they have ordered them, with minimal delay between a customer placing their order and receiving it. For McDonald's this means the food is not cooked or assembled until a customer order has been received.

Previously, before the JIT system was introduced, the most popular items were cooked and kept hot under heat lamps for a specified amount of time before being sold. Any that were not sold in this time were thrown away after the time had expired.

### Questions

1 Explain how the JIT system improves the quality of food.
2 Explain how the JIT system helps to reduce costs.
3 State one disadvantage of the JIT system.

# 2.3 The skills and techniques of preparation, cooking and presentation of dishes

## What will I learn?

In this topic you will gain knowledge and understanding of the following areas:

2.3.1 How to prepare and make dishes
2.3.2 Presentation techniques
2.3.3 Food safety practices

---

### Getting started

Discuss the skills and techniques you could show when using the following foods:

- poultry
- meat
- fish
- eggs
- dairy products
- flour
- fruit and vegetables
- soya products.

---

## 2.3.1 How to prepare and make dishes

When selecting dishes to produce it is important to know the types of skills and skill levels required. Some dishes call for more complex skills than others. For Unit 2, you will need to demonstrate a range of food preparation, cooking and presentation techniques used in the production of dishes.

## Preparation techniques

In this unit, preparation and cooking techniques are categorised according to whether they are:

- basic
- medium, or
- complex.

Ready-made or pre-prepared components used in the preparation and cooking of dishes are all classed as basic.

Table 2.7 shows how each preparation skill is categorised.

**Table 2.7 Preparation skills categorised by level of difficulty**

| Basic | Medium | Complex |
|---|---|---|
| Blending | Creaming | Crimping |
| Beating | Dehydrating | Laminating (pastry) |
| Grating | Folding | Melting using a bain-marie |
| Hydrating | Kneading | Piping |
| Juicing | Measuring | Shaping |

| Basic | Medium | Complex |
|---|---|---|
| Marinating | Mixing | Unmoulding |
| Mashing | Puréeing | Whisking (aeration) |
| Melting | Rub-in | |
| Proving | Rolling | |
| Shredding | Skinning | |
| Sieving | Toasting (nuts/seeds) | |
| Tenderising | Weighing | |
| Zesting | | |

# Basic-skill preparation techniques

## Blending

**Blending** means to mix together two or more ingredients. This can be done by hand, using a hand blender (liquidiser) or in a food processor. An example of a dish prepared using blending is a coulis, which is a thick sauce made from blended cooked or raw fruit. It is then used to decorate a sweet dish; sometimes it is poured in an attractive shape at the side of a dessert, such as cheesecake, or served separately as a sauce.

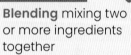

**Key terms**

**Blending** mixing two or more ingredients together

**Beating** combining ingredients together thoroughly

▲ **Using a hand blender**

## Beating

**Beating** means to combine ingredients together thoroughly, usually by mixing with a utensil such as a wooden spoon or spatula, or with an electric mixer. Foods are beaten to make them light and fluffy by the addition of air, for example when making a sponge cake or a batter.

## Grating

**Grating** is to make into coarse or fine threads by repeatedly rubbing an ingedient over one of the sides of a grater. A grater has small sharp-edged holes of different sizes and shapes. Examples include grating carrots or onions for a salad, or grating the zest of a lemon into fine fragments.

## Hydrating

**Hydrating** is adding water to an ingredient, which the ingredient then absorbs. Ingredients such as eggs and mushrooms can be bought dried; water is then added to the dried product to make it useable. Dried beans and peas need to be hydrated by soaking them in cold water for a few hours before they are used.

▲ **Dried beans need to be hydrated before they are used**

## Juicing

**Juicing** means to extract the juice from a fruit or vegetable, for example an orange or lemon.

## Marinating

A marinade is highly seasoned liquid that is used to give flavour, keep food moist and assist in tenderising foods. The liquid can be acidic, alkaline or a salt solution.

**Marinating** means to soak foods, such as fish, meat, poultry or vegetables, in a marinade to help develop their flavour, tenderise them and, in some instances, to colour the food before it is cooked. The marinade ingredients soften the proteins on the surface of meat, making it more tender. The marinated meat is then cooked, usually by barbecuing, grilling or roasting. During cooking, the marinade can also be used to baste the food, or it can be cooked separately in a saucepan to make an accompanying sauce.

Marinades suitable for vegetables and meat alternatives can be made from a variety of ingredients such as oil, wine, vinegar, soy sauce, garlic, herbs and spices.

The marinades add flavour to the food as well as moisture when the liquid is absorbed. Tofu and Quorn™ readily absorb flavours from other ingredients. Fruit can also be marinated.

## Mashing

**Mashing** is to reduce a food to a soft mass using a masher or a ricer (for example using a masher to make mashed potato).

## Melting

**Melting** is a method that uses heat to change a solid ingredient to a liquid. Some cakes are made by the melting method, with ingredients such as butter, syrup, sugar or treacle placed in a saucepan on a low heat until they melt. Chocolate is melted to make decorations or to add to recipes such as brownies.

▲ **Melting butter**

## Proving

**Proving** is leaving a dough, such as bread dough, to rise before baking.

## Shredding

**Shredding** is to slice into long thin strips (for example cabbage is shredded to make coleslaw).

## Sieving

**Sieving** is to pass an ingredient, such as icing sugar or flour, through a wire or plastic mesh sieve. This will remove lumps and will also add air. Ingredients such as cocoa and icing sugar can be sieved together so that they are evenly distributed in a cake or biscuit mixture.

Soups, such as tomato soup, can be sieved after blending to remove the pips and skin.

**Key terms**

**Mashing** reducing a food to a soft mass using a masher or ricer

**Melting** using heat to change a solid ingredient into a liquid

**Proving** leaving a dough, such as bread, to rise before baking

**Shredding** slicing into long thin strips

**Sieving** passing an ingredient through a wire or plastic mesh sieve

▲ **Sieving removes lumps and adds air**

### Tenderising

**Tenderising** meat and poultry is a process by which the tough muscle fibres are broken down in order to make the meat more tender.

Meat can be tenderised in three different ways:
1 by cooking it at a low temperature for a long time
2 by mechanical action – physically breaking down the muscle fibres by pounding them with a hammer, mincing or cutting larger pieces of meat into chunks
3 chemically, by marinating – with, for example, the addition of fruit such as kiwi, pineapple or papaya, or natural yoghurt.

### Zesting

Zest is the coloured outer skin of citrus fruits. It can be removed by **zesting**. Zesting can be done using a fine grater, or a zester can be used; this is a small utensil specifically designed to remove the zest only.

## Medium-skill preparation techniques

### Creaming

**Creaming** is beating ingredients together to incorporate air. The creaming method is used to make many cakes, including Victoria sandwich cakes.

#### *Creaming method*
1 Beat the fat and sugar together until the mixture is light and fluffy.
2 Lightly beat the eggs in a separate small bowl.
3 Beat the eggs into the fat and sugar mixture a little at a time.
4 Fold in the flour with a metal spoon.*

(*Folding is explained below.)

## Dehydrating

Food can be dehydrated to gently preserve nutrients and flavours by drying the food at low temperatures. Dehydration is also a method by which food can be preserved or used in a dry form when the moisture has been removed (see page 175).

## Folding

**Folding** is to stir a whisked or beaten mixture very gently to retain as much air as possible. It is best done with a metal spoon in a figure-of-eight action, or by moving around the bowl and cutting across the middle.

## Kneading

**Kneading** is pushing, pulling and folding bread dough until it becomes smooth and silky.

Gluten is formed when the two proteins in flour mix with water. Gluten is responsible for the elastic texture of dough and is important in creating the structure of bread. If dough is not kneaded enough, it will not be able to hold the tiny pockets of carbon dioxide created by the yeast. Kneading warms and stretches the gluten strands, eventually creating a springy, elastic dough. It can be done by hand on a lightly floured surface or in a food mixer using a dough hook.

## Measuring

Assessing ingredients by volume is called **measuring**. Most recipes depend on accurate measurement for their success, so it is important to be able to measure accurately.

A measuring jug is used to measure liquids; the side of the jug is usually marked with millilitres, litres/fluid ounces or both. Measuring spoons are very useful for measuring an accurate teaspoon or tablespoon: 1 teaspoon is 5 ml, 1 tablespoon is 15 ml.

▲ **Measuring equipment**

## Mixing

**Mixing** is the process of combining two or more ingredients to become one. For example, when making a Victoria sandwich cake, the butter and sugar are mixed together (creamed) with a wooden spoon or electric hand whisk to combine them.

Most recipes require you to combine or mix the ingredients in some way so that they blend together. Combining is similar to mixing. The instruction 'combine all the ingredients' may also specify 'thoroughly' or 'gently', depending on what is required to achieve the desired end result.

Equipment used to mix includes spoons, spatulas, whisks, processors and blenders.

## Puréeing

**Puréeing** means to make a smooth mixture of food. This is often done with an electric blender or can be done by pushing the food through a sieve.

## Rub-in

**Rub-in** (also known as rubbing in) is using your fingertips to rub fat into flour. This traps air in the mixture and coats the flour with a waterproof layer of fat. This prevents the gluten from developing too much in order to ensure a light, crumbly texture. The rubbing-in method is used to make rock cakes, scones, crumbles and pastry.

## Rolling

**Rolling** is to spread out or flatten. Various ingredients can be rolled to create dishes.

Shortcrust pastry is rolled out before use. When rolling the pastry, use a rolling pin and roll with firm, even strokes.

Pastry should be rolled in one direction so as not to distort the pastry shape, and it should be moved a few degrees regularly as you roll.

Pastry is rolled on a lightly floured surface to stop it from sticking.

▲ **Rolled pastry**

Other ingredients, such as bread dough and biscuit dough, can be rolled out, filled and then rolled up into a sausage and cut into slices to make pinwheel shapes.

A Swiss roll is a whisked cake that can be spread with jam and rolled up. It is essential to work quickly when making a Swiss roll because the cake can only be rolled successfully when it is still warm; it may crack if the cake cools. Roulades are another example of a rolled dish.

### Key terms

**Mixing** the process of combining two or more ingredients to become one

**Puréeing** making a food into a smooth mixture

**Rub-in** using the fingertips to combine ingredients, for example rubbing fat into flour to make pastry

**Rolling** spreading out or flattening

## Skinning

**Skinning** means to remove the skin from a food item. The skin of peaches and tomatoes can be removed by placing them in a bowl of boiling water. Peppers can be skinned by placing them on direct heat.

The skin of fish and poultry can also be removed by skinning. Removing skin from chicken can be done using the fingers, a knife or scissors.

When skinning fish, hold the tail end of the fish firmly and make a small cut through, with the knife moving away from you as you cut the flesh from the skin in a sawing action.

## Toasting (nuts/seeds)

**Toasting** means to cook or to brown food by direct heat (also called radiation). Nuts and seeds are toasted to bring out their flavour and release their oils. Toasting also has the effect of making them crunchier. Nuts and seeds can be toasted in the oven or in a dry frying pan.

## Weighing

**Weighing** is to measure ingredients by weight. Most recipes depend on accurate measurements for their success, so it is important to be able to weigh accurately. When making a cake, if you add too much sugar or flour the results are likely to be poor. However, in some recipes, such as a Bolognese sauce, it does not matter if you put in two onions instead of one.

The following equipment is useful for weighing:
- kitchen scales – digital/electronic kitchen scales are most widely used
- measuring cups – some American recipes use cups to measure dried ingredients such as flour and sugar; cups should not be used to weigh fat
- measuring spoons – these are very useful for measuring an accurate teaspoon or tablespoon (1 teaspoon is 5 ml, 1 tablespoon is 15 ml).

**Key terms**

**Skinning** removing the skin from a food

**Toasting** cooking or browning food using direct heat, such as a grill, toaster or open fire

**Weighing** measuring ingredients by weight

**Crimping** pressing a decorative pattern into the edge of a pie crust before it is baked (sometimes called fluting)

### Activity

Name a suitable dish for each of the medium-skill preparation techniques discussed above. For example:
- Rolling – making a quiche using shortcrust pastry

# Complex-skill preparation techniques

## Crimping

**Crimping** (sometimes known as fluting) means to press a decorative pattern into the edge of pastry before it is baked. There are three methods of crimping:
1. use a fork and press it into the edge of the pie crust
2. use two hands to pinch the edge of the crust; push your thumb from one hand in between the thumb and index finger of your other hand
3. use one hand to pinch the edge of the crust between your thumb and the side of your index finger on the same hand.

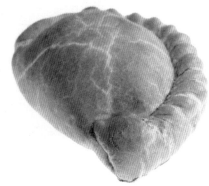

▲ **Pastry crimped to form the edge of a Cornish pasty**

## Laminating (pastry)

When making flaky pastry, the dough is rolled then butter is added and the dough is folded; this is repeated many times to create very thin layers in the pastry. This process is called **laminating**. It makes the texture very light as air is trapped between the many layers. The following baked items rely on lamination for their texture:

- croissants
- Danish pastries
- flaky pastry
- puff pastry
- parathas.

## Melting using a bain-marie

When **melting using a bain-marie** a saucepan is filled with about 4 cm of water then placed over a medium heat until it is simmering gently. A heatproof bowl is placed on top so it fits tightly but is not touching the water. The heat can then be turned down or even off. The product that is to be melted is then placed in the bowl.

Chocolate is an example of a product that would be melted using a bain-marie. It is important not to overheat it and that the water does not touch the chocolate otherwise the chocolate will **seize**, which means that it becomes grainy and is then unusable.

## Piping

**Piping** is to press a soft ingredient, such as whipped cream or mashed potato, through a piping bag fitted with a shaped nozzle to produce a decorative shape, for example when butter icing is piped on top of a cupcake.

▲ **Piping butter icing on to cupcakes**

## Shaping

**Shaping** is modelling food to create an attractive form. Shaping can either be done by hand or using a machine. Examples of shaping are:

- making burgers, koftas or meatballs
- making sugarcraft decorations
- making biscuits using a cutter
- making choux pastry using a piping bag.

Some food can be moulded into a shape by manipulating it (for example marzipan or fondant icing). Rice can be placed into a ring and pressed firmly to create a more interesting shape. A quenelle is an egg-shaped portion of food, such as ice cream or whipped cream; the shape is created by scooping a soft, smooth food using two spoons.

▲ **Whisked egg whites**

## Unmoulding

Food that has been set in a mould can be **unmoulded** by turning it out (for example panna cotta, jelly, blancmange).

## Whisking (aeration)

**Whisking** is when a food is beaten vigorously to trap air into it. This process is called **aeration**. A number of pieces of equipment can be used to whisk:

- fork
- balloon whisk
- electric hand mixer
- free-standing mixer.

Eggs and cream are commonly whisked as both ingredients trap air. Whisking makes the protein in the egg or cream unravel, which allows tiny air bubbles to be incorporated. This makes the mixture light and fluffy.

**Key terms**

**Shaping** modelling food to create an attractive form

**Unmoulding** turning a food out of a mould

**Whisking** (aeration) when a food is beaten vigorously to trap air into it

**Aeration** adding air to a mixture by beating or whisking it vigorously

**Activity**

Name a suitable dish for each of the complex-skill preparation techniques discussed above. For example:

■ Whisking – making a pavlova

## Extension activity

Find some recipes that use more than one complex-skill preparation technique. For example:

■ Cream horns – making puff pastry and piping cream

The whisking method is used to make Swiss rolls, sponge sandwich cakes and sponge flan cases. Sponges are cakes that contain no fat, which means that they soon become stale and should be eaten within a day of being made. The ingredients used in a sponge are flour, eggs and caster sugar. Self-raising flour can be used to give extra lightness, although plain flour could be used. In recipes made using the whisking method it is important to sieve the flour to add extra air.

### Basic whisking method

1 Put the eggs and sugar into a mixing bowl.
2 Using an electric mixer, whisk until they are thick, white and creamy. Test carefully to see if the mixture is ready. It should hold the mark of the beater trailed over the mixture for at least 10 seconds. This is called 'ribbon texture'.
3 Using a metal spoon, gently fold the sieved flour into the mixture a little at a time. This must be done very lightly and carefully, but thoroughly.
4 Pour the mixture into a prepared tin and bake in a fairly hot oven, about 200°C.

# Knife techniques

Table 2.8 shows how each knife technique is categorised.

**Table 2.8 Knife techniques categorised by level of difficulty**

| Basic | Medium | Complex |
|---|---|---|
| Chopping | Bâton | Brunoise |
| Peeling | Chiffonade | Deboning |
| Trimming | Deseeding | Filleting |
| | Dicing | Julienne |
| | Slicing | Mincing |
| | Spatchcock | Segmenting |

## Basic-skill knife techniques

### Chopping

▲ **The bridge hold and the claw grip**

**Chopping** means cutting food into small pieces of roughly the same size.

There are two techniques for holding, chopping and slicing foods such as fruit and vegetables: bridge hold and claw grip.

- Bridge hold:
  - use your thumb and forefinger and grip either side of the ingredient
  - use the knife to slice the ingredient in the gap underneath the bridge formed by your finger and thumb.
- Claw grip:
  - with the tips of your fingers and thumb tucked under towards the palm of your hand, hold the ingredient to be cut in a claw-like grip
  - hold the knife in your other hand, carefully bringing it across to slice the ingredient.

## Peeling

**Peeling** is to remove a thin layer of the skin of fruits and vegetables using a peeler or knife (for example taking the skin off potatoes). A peeler is often used in this process.

▲ Peeling

## Trimming

**Trimming** is to remove the visible fat from meat. A cooked pastry case can also be trimmed. Leave about a 1 cm overlap when making a pastry case and curl it over the edge of the tin. This will allow for shrinkage and enable you to trim the pastry using a sharp knife once it is cooked.

> ### Key terms
>
> **Chopping** cutting food into small pieces of roughly the same size
>
> **Peeling** removing a thin layer of the skin of fruit and vegetables using a peeler or knife
>
> **Trimming** removing the visible fat from meat, or excess pastry

▲ Trimming pastry

## Activity

Name a suitable dish for each of the basic-skill knife techniques discussed above. For example:
- Peeling – peeling a potato to make duchesse potatoes

▲ Cutting vegetables into bâtons (jardinière)

## Medium–skill knife techniques

### Bâton

This means cutting vegetables into short, thick batons. Another name for **bâton** is jardinière. To do this:

1 cut the vegetables into 1.5 cm lengths
2 cut these lengthways into 3 mm slices
3 cut the slices into bâtons.

### Chiffonade

**Chiffonade** is a roll-slicing action used to cut soft, delicate foods such as lettuce, or green vegetables such as cabbage, into ribbons. Place several leaves on top of one another then roll them into a cigar shape, hold the rolled leaves tightly and cut.

### Deseeding

**Deseeding** means to remove seeds before use (for example deseeding a red pepper).

## Dicing

**Dicing** is to cut fruits or vegetables into small cube shapes.

## Slicing

**Slicing** is to cut a thin, broad piece from a larger piece of food (for example a slice of cheese or bread) or to cut a wedge-shaped piece of food from a larger circular piece (for example a slice of pizza, cake or pie).

## Spatchcock

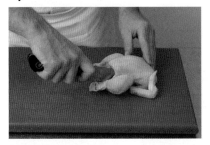  

▲ **Preparing a spatchcock chicken**

To **spatchcock** is to take a small chicken or any other bird and split it in half by removing the backbone so it is flattened. It can then be barbecued or grilled.

### Activity

Name a suitable dish for each of the medium-skill knife techniques. For example:
- Deseeding – a red pepper to make stuffed peppers

## Complex-skill knife techniques

### Brunoise

**Brunoise** means cutting vegetables into tiny dice from julienne strips (see below).

▲ **Brunoise**

**Key terms**

**Dicing** cutting fruit or vegetables into small cube shapes

**Slicing** cutting a thin or broad piece from a larger piece of food (for example a slice of bread) or cutting a wedge-shaped piece of food from a larger circular piece (for example a slice of pizza)

**Spatchcock** to split a small chicken, or any other bird, in half by removing the backbone so it is flattened; it can then be barbecued or grilled

**Brunoise** cutting vegetables into tiny dice from julienne strips

## Deboning

To **debone** means to remove the bones from a joint of meat, poultry or fish. Often food is deboned to prepare it for stuffing.

▲ **Example of deboning**

## Filleting

Chicken can be bought whole or in portions (pieces). It is possible to cut a whole chicken into portions. This process is also called jointing. When just the breast is removed from the chicken this is called **filleting**.

A fish **fillet** is a cut of fish that is free from bones. You can get two fillets from a round fish such as salmon, and four fillets from a flat fish such as Dover sole.

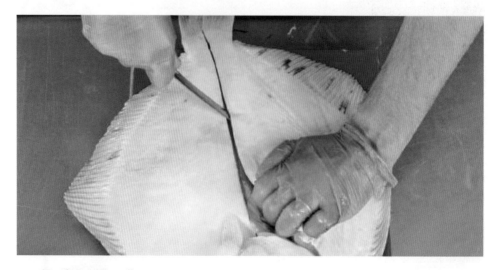

▲ **Filleting a flat fish**

## Filleting a round fish

1 Remove the head and clean the fish thoroughly.
2 Using a filleting knife, cut the flesh along the line of the backbone and raise the fillet from the middle of the back to the sides, working from head to tail.
3 Reverse the fish and remove the second fillet from tail to head.
4 After both fillets have been removed, remove the rib cavity bones and trim the fish neatly.

▲ **Remove the head and clean thoroughly**

▲ **Remove the first fillet by cutting along the backbone from head to tail; then, keeping the knife close to the bone, remove the fillet**

▲ **Once both fillets have been removed, remove the rib cavity bones and trim the fish neatly**

## Julienne

**Julienne** means cutting vegetables into matchstick strips.

▲ **Julienne**

## Mincing

**Mincing** means to reduce food to very small pieces. This can be done using a knife or a mincing machine. Meats such as beef, pork, lamb, chicken and turkey can be minced successfully.

**Key terms**

**Julienne** cutting vegetables into matchstick-shaped strips

**Mincing** reducing food to very small pieces

▲ **Segmenting an orange**

## Segmenting

**Segmenting** means to divide into pieces (for example in the case of an orange or grapefruit).

### Activity

Name a suitable dish for each of the medium-skill knife techniques. For example:

- Julienne – stir-fry vegetables

# Cooking techniques

Table 2.9 shows how each cooking skill is categorised.

**Table 2.9 Cooking techniques categorised by level of difficulty**

| Basic | Medium | Complex |
|---|---|---|
| Basting | Baking | Baking blind |
| Boiling | Blanching | Caramelising |
| Chilling | Braising | Deep fat frying |
| Cooling | Deglazing | Emulsifying |
| Dehydrating | Frying | Poaching |
| Freezing | Griddling | Tempering |
| Grilling | Pickling | |
| Skimming | Reduction | |
| Toasting | Roasting | |
| | Sautéing | |
| | Setting | |
| | Steaming | |
| | Stir-frying | |
| | Water bath (sous-vide) | |

## Basic-skill cooking techniques

### Basting

**Basting** means to spoon over stock or fat during cooking to stop food from drying out. Basting also helps the food to brown. Roast meat is basted with hot fat regularly during cooking.

### Boiling

**Boiling** is a method of cooking where foods are cooked in boiling water or other liquid, which makes them tender. Water boils at 100°C; when it is boiling you can see bubbles and the water moves. The most commonly used liquids in which to boil food are:

- water
- milk
- stock.

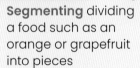

### Key terms

**Segmenting** dividing a food such as an orange or grapefruit into pieces

**Basting** spooning over stock or fat during cooking to stop food from drying out and to help it to brown

**Boiling** cooking food in boiling water or other liquid to make it tender

There are two methods of boiling:

1 The liquid should be placed in a saucepan on the highest heat until it boils. Add the food when the water is boiling. Cover the pan with a tightly fitting lid to keep the heat in, then time the cooking of the food as required. The heat can then be reduced slightly.

2 Cover the food with cold liquid, heat it up to boiling point then reduce the heat slightly once boiling.

Care needs to be taken when boiling because the food may disintegrate if it is boiled for too long. It is a good idea to use the liquid that food has been boiled in to make stock or a sauce.

- Boiling is a healthy method of cooking because no fat is used.
- All pieces of food being boiled should be of the same size to ensure it all cooks at the same time.
- The amount of liquid used varies; a general rule is that it should cover the food completely but use the minimum amount possible for vegetables.
- The opposite is true for pasta, where there should be more water so that the pasta can move around in it.
- Older, tougher and, therefore, cheaper cuts of meat can be boiled gently to make them tastier and more tender.
- Foods suitable for boiling include whole eggs, gammon, jam, rice, pasta and stock.

## Chilling

**Chilling** means keeping food cool to stop harmful bacteria from growing. Chilled food should be kept in the fridge at between 0°C and below 5°C to keep it safe. This applies to:

- food with a 'use by' date
- cooked dishes
- other ready-to-eat food, such as prepared salads and desserts.

## Cooling

**Cooling** is when the temperature of food is reduced. Food that is not going to be eaten straight away is cooled to be eaten cold or reheated later. Food should be cooled to 5°C or below within 90 minutes to keep it out of the temperature danger zone. (For more information on the temperature danger zone see page 103.) Blast chillers cool food rapidly by moving very cold air around the food.

## Dehydrating

**Dehydrating** is when the moisture is removed from food to preserve it. It can be rehydrated or used in powder form to flavour food (for example raspberry powder, which can be used when making meringues). Fruit and vegetables can be dried and used to garnish foods. Fruits such as bananas, apples and mangoes can be dehydrated successfully.

## Freezing

Freezers store food for longer periods of time than a fridge. The food in a freezer is stored at −18°C or colder. At this temperature, bacteria do not have the warmth they need to grow and cannot multiply. As well as having no warmth, they have no water as it has turned into ice, which makes water unavailable to the micro-organisms.

**Key terms**

**Chilling** keeping food cool to prevent the growth of harmful bacteria by placing it in a fridge

**Cooling** reducing the temperature of food

**Dehydrating** (of food) removing the moisture from food, for example drying it at a low temperature, to preserve it

## Key terms

**Freezing** storing food at a temperature of –18°C or colder

**Grilling** a dry method of cooking food by applying heat to its surface

Most bacteria survive the **freezing** process. While they are in the freezer, they become dormant, which means they are inactive. Once the food is defrosted (thawed), the bacteria can multiply again. Defrosted food should be treated in the same way as fresh food and consumed as soon as possible.

Foods may be stored in the freezer for up to one year, depending on the type of food. Foods that are frozen for too long are still safe to eat, but their flavour and texture will deteriorate over time. Commercially bought frozen food will have a 'best before' date that should be followed.

## Grilling

**Grilling** is a method of cooking food by applying heat to the surface of the food. Grilling is a useful method of cooking because it is quick. It is also healthy because it does not need fat and, if the food being grilled contains fat, some of it drains away as it is cooked. Grilled food has a distinctive appearance and flavour. The food being grilled is visible during cooking, which makes it easier to check whether it is cooked or not.

▲ **Grilling cheese on toast**

Grilling under heat is achieved by using the grill section of an ordinary cooker. Grills have a variable control so you can select the heat you require according to your recipe. They also have multi-position shelves with a higher and lower position to get the right distance between the grill and the food. Most cookers come with a grill pan and a handle, which is often detachable. This means the pan can be pulled out from under the grill, the food checked and turned, and the pan slid back under the grill. Some cooker manufacturers recommend grilling with the door open, others with the door closed. It is important to follow their instructions for safety reasons.

Foods suitable for grilling include:

- meat – best-quality tender meat such as steak, lamb and pork chops, chicken breasts, burgers and sausages
- vegetables – tomatoes, mushrooms, thick slices of onion
- fish – fish fingers, cod steaks, tuna steaks
- cheese – halloumi works very well when grilled as it holds its shape
- seeds and nuts – many seeds and nuts, such as hazelnuts, almonds, coconut and sesame seeds, can be toasted under the grill; they cook extremely quickly so need to be watched carefully and moved around to ensure even cooking
- breads – croissants, brioche and bread slices can be toasted on each side using a grill to crisp and brown the outside; naan bread can be cooked by grilling the prepared and shaped dough.

## Skimming

**Skimming** is when excess fat and impurities are removed with a slotted spoon. When making stock the fat should be skimmed off the top to leave a clear and non-greasy stock.

When making jam, impurities appear on the top. These can be removed by skimming.

## Toasting

Toasting is to cook food using a grill, toaster or open fire. This makes food brown and crispy. Bread is a commonly toasted food.

> **Activity**
>
> Name a suitable dish for each of the basic-skill cooking techniques discussed above. For example:
> - Basting – a baked ham with a honey glaze

# Medium-skill cooking techniques

## Baking

**Baking** is cooking food in a hot oven without adding extra fat during the cooking process. When baking, it is important that the oven is preheated, as baked food needs to be placed in a hot oven. If a baking tin is being used, it is important to check that it will fit in the oven. It should not touch the sides of the oven as this may prevent the hot air from circulating.

A range of foods can be baked, including cakes, biscuits, scones, pastry, vegetables, fish, puddings, desserts, fruit and pre-prepared products.

## Blanching

**Blanching** is a method of cooking where food is cooked very quickly in boiling water for a short period of time and then cooled quickly to stop the cooking process.

> **Key terms**
>
> **Skimming** removing excess fat and impurities (for example from a stock) using a slotted spoon
>
> **Baking** cooking food in a hot oven without adding extra fat during the cooking process
>
> **Blanching** when food is cooked very quickly in boiling water then cooled to stop the cooking process

Blanching can be used in several ways:

- to remove the skin from fruit and vegetables (for example peaches or tomatoes)
- chips can be blanched and then fried later; this will make them fluffy inside and crisp on the outside
- chefs often blanch vegetables and then plunge them into cold water to stop the cooking process; these vegetables can then be reheated very quickly when needed without losing their colour or shape
- vegetables and fruits are blanched before freezing to help keep their colour and to destroy enzymes that would spoil them.

### How to blanch vegetables

1 Wash, peel, trim and cut the vegetables into the same size and shape.
2 Bring enough water to the boil to cover the vegetables.
3 Add the vegetables to the water.
4 Cook the vegetables until they are the required texture – one or two minutes is usually enough.
5 Drain the vegetables.
6 Place the vegetables in cold water to stop the cooking process.

The vegetables can then be used in a variety of ways. For example:

- shallow-fried (for example sauté potatoes)
- in a sauce (for example a vegetable bake or vegetables in a white sauce)
- griddled (for example asparagus).

## Braising

**Braising** is a moist method of cooking used for larger pieces of food. The food is only half covered with a liquid and is then cooked slowly for a long time at a low temperature. Usually a pan with a tight-fitting lid is used for braising. The food can be braised either on the hob or in the oven. A range of foods can be braised, including meat, vegetables and rice.

Rice works well when braised and is called pilaf. By braising the rice instead of boiling it, less water is used: the exact amount of water for the rice to absorb is added and there is then no need to drain away excess water.

## Deglazing

**Deglazing** loosens the browned juices, usually from meat, on the bottom of the pan by adding a liquid such as stock or wine to the hot pan and stirring while the liquid is boiling. This creates a gravy/sauce that can be served with the food.

## Frying

**Frying** is a quick method of cooking where a small amount of fat is used to cook food in a frying pan. The fat should come only about halfway up the food. The food is in direct contact with the fat so it cooks quickly. This method of cooking adds flavour and moisture to the food and stops it from sticking to the frying pan.

- Oil can be used for frying, as it can be heated successfully to a high temperature.
- Butter can be used for frying, but care needs to be taken because it burns easily.
- If a mixture of butter and oil is used, you get the flavour of butter but the oil will prevent the butter from burning.

### Key terms

**Braising** a moist method of cooking used for larger pieces of food, when the food is only half covered with a liquid and cooked slowly for a long time at a low temperature

**Deglazing** loosening the browned juices on the bottom of a pan by adding a liquid to the hot pan and stirring as the liquid boils

**Frying** a fast method of cooking using a small amount of fat to cook food in a frying pan

▲ **Shallow-frying eggs**

It is important that the fat is heated before the food that is going to be fried is added so that a crust will form on the food, preventing it from absorbing too much fat and becoming too greasy. Fried food has a distinctive flavour: it is crispy and browned on the outside. All foods need to be turned so they are cooked and browned on both sides. Foods suitable for frying include eggs, burgers, fishcakes, sausages and bacon.

## Griddling

**Griddling** is grilling over heat and can be achieved by using a chargrill, where grill bars are heated from underneath. The heat comes from either gas, electricity or charcoal. Griddling can also be achieved by cooking with a griddle pan, which gives the food (for example steak, tuna, halloumi cheese) an attractive griddled effect.

> **Key term**
>
> **Griddling** cooking over heat using a chargrill or griddle pan

▲ **Using a griddle pan**

## Pickling

**Pickling** is a way to preserve foods that uses an acidic solution such as vinegar. Many micro-organisms cannot live in acidic conditions and so acids help to preserve the food. Onions, for example, can be preserved by pickling in vinegar.

## Reduction

**Reduction** is when a liquid is simmered over heat so that the water content evaporates, resulting in a more concentrated liquid. This process thickens and intensifies the flavour of the liquid. Reduction sauces can be made from the cooking liquid in which meat, fish or vegetables have been cooked, or by deglazing the brown sediment from the bottom of pan with water, stock or wine following pan-frying. Making reduction sauces takes time – some can take up to an hour. The time needed will depend on how much liquid has been used.

## Roasting

**Roasting** is cooking and browning with the aid of fat. Roasted foods have a good flavour and an attractive crisp appearance. Meat is roasted by quickly sealing it first to keep the juices in. This process is called **searing** and is where the outside of the meat is cooked quickly on a high heat to form a crust and to keep the meat juices inside. It can then be placed in the oven to continue cooking, and should be basted regularly with hot fat throughout the cooking process.

A range of food can be roasted, for example beef, lamb, pork and chicken, and vegetables such as potatoes, parsnips and mixed vegetables (such as peppers, onions and tomatoes).

## Sautéing

**Sautéing** is to cook food in fat. Sautéing is done at a higher temperature than frying because the food is cooked quickly, and a deeper pan is needed because the food being sautéed should be stirred regularly. Food being sautéed is usually cut into smaller pieces. Foods suitable for sautéing include chicken and potatoes.

## Setting

**Setting** is when a liquid becomes firmer. Starches such as cornflour, when heated with a liquid, will thicken a mixture. This process is called **gelatinisation**. This mixture can then be chilled and it will set, which is called **gelation**. Gelatinisation occurs when starch granules are mixed with a liquid and heated, which makes them swell and break open, causing the liquid to thicken. Gelation is when a mixture is thickened by starch and sets on chilling.

One example of using the gelation process is when commercially bought custard powder is mixed with milk and heated. The custard thickens and will set on chilling; it can then be used as one of the layers in a trifle or to make blancmange.

## Steaming

**Steaming** is a method of cooking in which food is cooked in the steam coming off boiling water. The water is brought to the boil in a steamer or saucepan and the food is then placed in a steaming compartment above the water, or wrapped up tightly and placed in the water. Other liquids may be used to add flavour and moisture, such as stock and infused liquids (liquids with seasoning, spice, herbs or wine added).

It is difficult to overcook steamed food; it remains soft and will not become crispy or dry out. As no water comes into direct contact with the food, there is little nutrient loss. No fat is used, so it is a healthy method of cooking, especially for vegetables. Sponge puddings can be steamed and, due to the steam, are much lighter in texture than baked sponges.

When opening a steamer, take care to let some steam escape before you look at or lift out the food.

There are several different ways in which food can be steamed:

- plate method – putting the food between two plates on top of a pan of boiling water
- saucepan method – placing food in a container or bowl in a saucepan of boiling water; the water must come halfway up the container
- tiered steamer – using a tiered steamer pan on top of a saucepan containing boiling water
- electric steamer – this works like a tiered steamer but electricity is used to heat the water in the bottom layer rather than a saucepan on the hob.

▲ **An electric steamer**

Whichever method is used, it is important not to let the water boil dry. Check it and top up when necessary.

Foods suitable for steaming include potatoes, vegetables, sponges and fish.

## Stir-frying

**Stir-frying** is a quick method of cooking where small pieces of food are fried quickly in a small amount of oil, usually in a **wok** (a rounded frying pan). The wok and the oil must be hot before adding the food. All the food should be chopped and sliced finely to ensure that it is cooked evenly and quickly. The food should be moved around while cooking to ensure the heat is equally distributed, so the food cooks evenly. It is a good idea to stir-fry any meat first to ensure it is cooked thoroughly before adding vegetables.

Foods suitable for stir-frying include steak, pork tenderloin, chicken breast, vegetables and noodles.

**Key terms**

**Stir-frying** a quick method of cooking, where small pieces of food are fast-fried in a small amount of oil in a wok

**Wok** a rounded frying pan

▲ **Stir-frying**

## Water bath (sous-vide)

**Water bath (sous-vide)** is a method of cooking where food such as fish is cooked very slowly in a vacuum-packed pouch in a water bath at a low temperature. This helps reduce moisture loss and also allows the food to be cooked in a marinade or sauce.

**Activity**

Name a suitable dish for each of the medium-skill cooking techniques discussed above. For example:
■ Stir-fry – vegetable chow mein

# Complex-skill cooking techniques

## Baking blind

**Baking blind** means precooking pastry before a filling is added. To bake blind you need first to make a cartouche (a circle of parchment paper), a little bigger than the size of the pastry case. Line the pastry with the cartouche and then fill the pastry case with baking beans (small ceramic beans). This will prevent the pastry from rising. Once the pastry has been baked blind, the beans and cartouche need to be removed and the pastry placed back in the oven to dry out the base. This prevents the pastry base being soggy. Pastry cases for quiches and lemon tart are baked blind as part of the process.

▲ **Vacuum-packed sirloin steak being cooked in a water bath (sous-vide)**

▲ **Baking pastry blind**

## Caramelising

**Caramelising** is when sugar is cooked until it becomes a deep golden colour. The temperature at which sugar caramelises is 170°C. Wet caramel is made with sugar and water, and is used to make dishes such as oranges in caramel sauce. Dry caramel is when sugar is heated on its own and used to make decorations. It is also used as the topping for a crème brûlée.

# Deep fat frying

**Deep fat frying** is when small, tender pieces of food are immersed in very hot fat for a short period of time. It browns and crisps food, making it both attractive and appetising. It is, however, an unhealthy method of cooking due to the food absorbing fat when it cooks.

Great care needs to be taken when deep-frying because the temperature of the oil can reach 195°C. Hot fat can cause serious burns through spillages and accidents. In a catering kitchen, only trained staff are allowed to deep-fry.

Deep-frying is mostly done in commercial fryers that are thermostatically controlled, making them much safer. Most deep-frying is done in oil. Some food is coated (for example in batter, flour or breadcrumbs) before deep-frying to help seal it and protect its surface. Foods suitable for deep-frying include meat, poultry, vegetables, fish, fruit, onion bhajis, churros and doughnuts.

# Emulsifying

**Emulsifying** is the process by which two liquids that would not normally mix, such as oil and vinegar, are mixed together and an emulsion is formed. This emulsion can be 'stable' or 'unstable'. An example of a stable emulsion, which is where the mixture does not separate, is mayonnaise or hollandaise sauce. The emulsion is stable in this case because an emulsifying agent such as egg yolk is added. Examples of unstable emulsions, which is where the mixture does separate, are vinaigrette salad dressings made from oil and vinegar with no emulsifying agent.

# Poaching

**Poaching** is when food is cooked in a liquid that is just below boiling point. The poaching liquid is heated until it is not quite boiling, so just the occasional bubble can be seen. The food is then slowly lowered into the liquid and cooked very gently. It is necessary to control the heat carefully so that the liquid is not too cool but doesn't boil.

Poaching makes food tender; its flavour is enhanced in the cooking process because it is gentle and flavours are not lost as they would be during cooking at higher temperatures. It is a healthy method of cooking because few nutrients are lost and no fat is used.

The liquids that can be used for poaching are the same as those that can be used for boiling, but fruit can also be poached in wine (for example pears in red wine) or a syrup.

A saucepan or poaching pan is used, along with a slotted spoon to lift the poached food carefully out of the liquid. Foods suitable for poaching include chicken, fish such as salmon, eggs, and fruit such as pears.

# Tempering

**Tempering** is a method of heating then cooling chocolate to a specific temperature so that when the chocolate cools it has a glossy surface and will break with a sharp snap. Tempered chocolate is used for coating, chocolate decorations and making filled chocolates.

To temper chocolate it should be melted to a temperature of 45°C and then cooled to 27°C.

## Key terms

**Deep fat frying** cooking by immersing small, tender pieces of food in very hot fat for a short time

**Emulsifying** the process by which two liquids that would not normally mix are mixed together to form an emulsion

**Poaching** cooking food in a liquid that is just below boiling point

**Tempering** heating then cooling chocolate to a specific temperature so that when it cools it has a glossy surface and will break with a sharp snap

## Activity

Name a suitable dish for each of the complex-skill cooking techniques discussed above. For example:

■ Deep fat frying – churros

### Extension activity

Name a dish that uses more than one complex skill. For example, eggs Benedict.

## Knowledge check

1 List the seven complex preparation skills and, for each one, give an example of a recipe that uses the skill.
2 Explain why meat would be marinated.
3 Explain how to make a Victoria sandwich cake by the creaming method.
4 Describe how to roll shortcrust pastry successfully.
5 Explain why it is important to develop the gluten when kneading bread.
6 Describe the three ways pastry can be crimped.
7 Describe what chiffonade means and give an example of a food that can be prepared using this technique.
8 Name the six complex cooking techniques and, for each one, give an example of a recipe that uses the technique.
9 List five foods suitable for grilling.
10 Describe how to blanch vegetables.

## Activity

1 List the complex preparation and cooking skills.
2 Research a range of recipes that use these skills and make one in your next practical lesson.

## Case study

Birds Eye is a familiar brand of frozen food. Clarence Birdseye invented the fast-freezing process in 1934. He went on to invent the multiple-plate freezer, which enabled food to be frozen with much smaller ice crystals forming. The frozen pea was first introduced to the UK in 1938 and, in 1955, fish finger production began.

### Questions

Have a look at the Birds Eye website at www.birdseye.com and then answer the following questions.

1 How is Birds Eye adapting to current trends?
2 What is the company doing about sustainable eating?

### Further reading

www.bbc.com/future/article/20210701-the-hidden-history-of-the-peas-in-your-freezer

## 2.3.2 Presentation techniques

The presentation of food is extremely important. Food needs to look attractive to a customer. How the food tastes is, of course, crucial. It is essential that the chef tastes and seasons the food during the cooking process, and adds the necessary quantities of seasonings, herbs, spices, marinades, pastes and sauces.

# Creativity

There are many different ways in which chefs can prepare and present food creatively. Making food look attractive makes it more appealing to customers.

### Piping

Piping is a technique used to make food look more attractive (see page 166). Examples include piped potato on a fish pie, duchesse potatoes, butter icing piped on a cupcake and piped cream on a trifle.

▲ **Piped duchesse potatoes**

### Glazing

**Glazing** is a technique used to make food look shiny, such as fruit tarts glazed with jelly, a sponge flan with arrowroot glaze or egg brushed on to a pie before cooking.

### Blending

Blending means to mix two or more ingredients together. This can be done by hand, by using a hand blender (liquidiser) or a food processor. A coulis is a thick sauce made from puréed cooked or raw fruit. It can be used to decorate a sweet dish; sometimes it is poured into an attractive shape at the side of a dessert, such as cheesecake, or served separately as a sauce.

**Key term**

**Glazing** making a shiny surface on food to give it an attractive appearance

▲ **A vanilla cheesecake decorated with raspberry coulis**

## Shaping

Food can be moulded into a shape by manipulating it, for example marzipan or fondant icing. Food can also be placed in a mould and then turned out, as in the case of panna cotta, jelly and blancmange. Rice can also be placed into a ring and pressed firmly to create a more interesting shape. A quenelle is an egg-shaped portion of food, such as ice cream or whipped cream. The shape is made by scooping a soft, smooth food using two spoons.

▲ **Fruit crumble served with a quenelle of ice cream**

## Stenciling

A stencil can be used to sprinkle icing sugar on top of a cake in a specific pattern, or it can be used on drinks, such as cappuccino, where cocoa is shaken on the top of the coffee in a specific design. Stencils can also be used to create elaborate designs on cakes and biscuits, which can then be cut into the correct shape. It is possible to create your own shapes for biscuits by creating a cut-out of a shape and using it as a guide to cut around.

## Layering

**Layering** means placing different foods on top of each other to create an attractive combination. When layering food, you should think about the colours and textures of each layer. Decide which layer will look best on the top. The texture of each layer is also important. Salads can be created in layers and a small amount of dressing will help them stick together. Trifle is an example of a layered dessert; it traditionally consists of sponge, fruit, custard and whipped cream.

▲ **A cake decorated with stencils**

▲ **A layered salad**

> ### Key terms
>
> **Layering** placing different foods on top of one another to create an attractive combination
>
> **Fluting** pressing a decorative pattern into the edge of a pie crust before it is baked (sometimes called crimping)

## Fluting

**Fluting** means to press a decorative pattern into the edge of a pie crust before it is baked. It is sometimes known as crimping. There are three methods of fluting:

1 use a fork and press it into the edge of the pie crust
2 use two hands to pinch the edge of the crust; push your thumb from one hand in between the thumb and index finger of your other hand
3 use one hand to pinch the edge of the crust between your thumb and the side of your index finger on the same hand.

▲ **A wedding cake decorated with fondant icing**

## Icing

Decorative icing can be used to enhance the appearance of large cakes, small cakes and biscuits. There are a number of techniques that can be used:

- glacé icing is a quick icing that can be made with icing sugar and water; it is often used for icing small cakes
- fondant icing can be made or bought ready to use; it is a moulding icing that can be used to make decorations, flowers, figures and animals to decorate cakes; it can also be used to cover a whole cake, providing a smooth, flat surface for decorating on
- royal icing is made from egg white and icing sugar; it is a traditional icing often used for covering cakes for weddings and Christmas; it can be spread or piped into shapes using different styles of nozzle
- butter icing is made from butter and icing sugar beaten together; it can be spread or piped into shapes using different styles of nozzle
- chocolate ganache is made from chocolate and cream; it can be used as a sauce, icing or glaze.

## Glazing

Decorative glazes are used to give desserts and cakes a shiny appearance. For example, fruit tarts can be glazed with sieved warmed apricot jam or redcurrant jelly. Arrowroot glaze can be used for desserts. It is made by blending arrowroot with water, bringing it to the boil so that the mixture thickens and then cools to a thick, clear glaze.

### Activity

Create a mood board of ideas for different ways to decorate cupcakes.

### Extension activity

Annotate the cupcakes with details of what icing/decorations are used.

# Plating techniques

When plating up food for serving there are many techniques that can be used to present the food attractively. It is always important to consider the following points:

- the style of serving dish, and how the food will be placed on the dish
- the centre height of the dish – food looks more attractive in a mound than flattened on a plate or serving dish
- if laying out a plate of biscuits or canapés, arrange them in contrasting rows, as this looks attractive

- overlap food, such as fruit slices or slices of meat, to stop it looking flat and dull on the plate
- keep colours to a minimum as lots of different colours can be overpowering; using two colours or different shades of a single colour works very successfully.

Sauces can be used to good effect in the presentation of food. They could be poured over the food, drizzled or dotted on it, or served in a small jug alongside the food.

Savoury food is often plated on oval dishes or plates, and sweet food on round plates or dishes. When plating cakes or biscuits, they can be placed on a doily, then a plate or tiered cake stand.

When plating up food to be served, particularly roast meals, the classical plating style can be used. This method of styling uses the idea of the plate being a clock:

- vegetables are placed between 12 and 3
- starchy foods are placed between 9 and 12
- the main component of the meal is placed between 3 and 9.

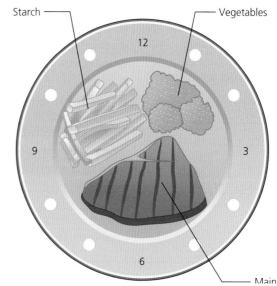

▲ **Plating food**

# Garnish and decoration

Adding an edible decoration to a finished dish can improve its appearance. Additions to savoury food dishes are called **garnishes**, while **decorations** added to sweet foods are simply called decorations. There are many techniques that can be used when preparing garnishes and decorations to make food look attractive.

▲ **A strawberry fan is an example of a decoration**

## Garnishing

Herbs are used for flavouring and to garnish foods. Herbs are the leaves and sometimes the stems of plants. They are sold both fresh, dried and frozen. Some are also puréed and sold in plastic packaging.

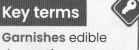

**Key terms**

**Garnishes** edible decorations on savoury food dishes

**Decorations** additions to sweet dishes to make them look more attractive; decorations are not always edible (for example sparklers or candles on a cake)

Some examples of herbs used for garnishing and how they might be used include:

- basil – the leaves are used to garnish pizzas and bruschetta
- chives – can be snipped using scissors (**scissor snipped**) over potatoes or fish
- coriander – the leaves are used to garnish curries and chiles
- mint – chopped and added to new potatoes
- parsley – used to garnish fish, vegetables and potatoes.

Table 2.10 **Techniques used in garnishing and decorating**

| Technique | Method |
|---|---|
| Fanning | A strawberry can be cut into slices with a knife, leaving the top of the strawberry intact, to create a fan effect; this can be used to decorate a cheesecake |
| 'Waterlily' effect | Using a knife, V-shaped notches are cut out around the edge to create a toothed effect; tomatoes and melon can be prepared in this way |
| Scoring with a fork | Score down with a sharp knife or fork to give ridged effect. Cucumber and lemons can be prepared in this way to make a salad garnish look more attractive |
| Twists | Cucumbers, oranges and lemons can be prepared in this way to decorate fish and salads – slice, then cut from the edge to just past the centre and twist to form a decorative shape |
| Ribbons | Courgettes or cucumbers can be peeled along their length to produce ribbons that can be arranged in different ways, for example making a spiral, folding or wrapping round another food such as a mousse |
| Curls | Placing cut vegetables in ice cold water can be very effective – radishes will open out in iced water and can then be cut through almost to the base; the green leaves of spring onions can be cut through into small strips while still attached to the root, and will curl if left in iced water; these can be used to garnish stir-fries or salads |

▲ **A dessert decorated with sugar work**

## Sugar work

Sugar can be used to make decorations. Sugar and water can be boiled to make spun sugar, which can then be manipulated into shapes. It can be wound round a handle of a wooden spoon to make a sugar spring or the sugar can be flicked across an upturned ladle and used to make a cage to decorate desserts.

# Chocolate work

Chocolate can be used in a variety of ways to enhance the appearance of cakes, biscuits and desserts. Chocolate curls can be made by using a vegetable peeler on chocolate that has been at room temperature. Chocolate work is mostly created with melted chocolate.

▲ **A dessert decorated with chocolate caraques**

There are a number of decorations you can make with melted chocolate:

■ chocolate leaves – brush the back of a clean leaf with melted chocolate; when the chocolate is dry, peel away the leaf

■ cut out shapes – spread the melted chocolate 3 mm thick on to waxed paper; leave to set then cut out using small cutters

■ chocolate scrolls – spread melted chocolate 3 mm thick on to waxed paper; leave to set then, using a long, firm knife, push across the chocolate at a slight angle to make scrolls (the same technique can be used to make chocolate caraques by holding the knife and pushing in a quarter-circle movement)

■ melted chocolate can also be piped into shapes, numbers and patterns and left to set.

**Activity**

Create a chocolate-themed mood board showing different ideas for dishes that include chocolate and dishes that show chocolate being used as a decoration.

▲ **The Korean *dalgona* coffee drink is topped with whipped iced coffee foam**

## Foams

Foams are aerated liquids; this means that they are liquids that have had air whisked in to them. The consistency of the foam will depend on the thickness of the liquid and the ratio of liquid to air. A lighter foam is sometimes described as froth – such as that on the top of a cappuccino – while a denser foam will look like a mousse. Whipped cream, meringue and mousse are all foams. They are all made by incorporating air and they all have a light texture. Foams can also be used to garnish dishes.

## Jus

A jus is a thin gravy or sauce that can be made from the juices of meat. It can be poured into a creative pattern on a plate to garnish the food.

# Portion control

Portion size or control means controlling the size or quantity of the food to be served to each customer. Controlling portion sizes will ensure that:

■ there is little wastage of food, which keeps costs down
■ customers have a consistent quantity of food, which will stop complaints about portion sizes
■ portions of food of the same size will cook at the same time.

There are a number of ways in which portion size can be controlled:

■ using scales to weigh foods such as steak
■ using a scoop, which would give a consistent number of portions of foods such as ice cream, sorbet and mashed potato
■ using a ladle to count out a portion of soup or sauces
■ fruit juice glasses can be used for measured drinks or jellies
■ using individual dishes for pies, pudding basins or moulds
■ marking the surface of a cake or dessert into sections so it is easy to see where to cut it accurately
■ using fruit such as strawberries to indicate portion size; for example, one strawberry = one portion
■ counting food, where appropriate (for example the number of biscuits included in cheese and biscuits).

▲ **Using a scoop to measure a portion of ice cream**

Table 2.11 gives examples of how many portions can be obtained from various foods to achieve consistent portion control in a restaurant.

Table 2.11 **Food portions**

| Food | Amount per one portion |
|------|------------------------|
| Steak | 125–250 g |
| Trout | 1 whole fish |
| Soup | 125 ml |
| Potatoes | 125 g |
| Salmon | 200 g |

# Accompaniments and side dishes

Accompaniments are foods served separately with a main meal. Some examples of accompaniments are:

■ roast beef – Yorkshire pudding, horseradish sauce
■ roast turkey – bread sauce, cranberry sauce, pigs in blankets.

Side dishes are extra dishes that go well with, and are often served with, a main meal. For example, at an Indian restaurant you could have a curry with a side dish of pilau rice, Bombay potatoes or lentil dhal. The side dishes for a roast beef main meal could be roast potatoes and vegetables.

## Knowledge check

1 What is meant by the term fluting?
2 Describe three different techniques for plating food.
3 Name a herb that can be chopped and added to new potatoes.

4 Give two reasons why accurate portion control is important to restaurants.
5 Name two traditional accompaniments to roast beef.

### Activity

Search YouTube for how to stencil cakes and watch some videos showing how to create effects.

### Extension activity

A fruit salad can be uninspiring. List some exotic fruit that could be used to make a fruit salad look more interesting, and come up with an original way of presenting or serving a fruit salad.

### Case study

Read the article written by Susan Johnston Taylor, where top chefs share ten food plating and presentation techniques, which can be found at this link: **www.lightspeedhq.co.uk/blog/10-food-plating-and-presentation-tips**.

### Question

Describe each plating technique and suggest foods that would be best suited to each technique. For example, when serving steak, cut the meat into slices and at an angle of 45 degrees.

# 2.3.3 Food safety practices

It is crucial to follow food safety practices when preparing food for a customer. The correct personal hygiene practices and food safety procedures should be followed when preparing and cooking food, and when using equipment and facilities.

Food safety and hygiene are very important when preparing food, to protect customers from contamination that may cause food poisoning. There are some basic rules that need to be followed to make sure food is not contaminated with biological (bacteria), physical or chemical hazards.

The following section describes the main situations where food could become contaminated. It is your responsibility to make sure you follow food safety rules to keep your customers safe.

# Personal hygiene for food workers

Personal hygiene is important for anyone preparing and cooking food. If high standards of personal hygiene are met, food poisoning is less likely to occur.

## Personal hygiene rules for the kitchen

- Don't cough or sneeze near food.
- Don't touch your head, especially your mouth, nose and ears.
- Don't brush your hair in the kitchen or while wearing your protective clothing.
- Long hair should be tied back or covered.
- Wounds, such as cuts and scratches, should be covered with a coloured waterproof plaster or dressing.
- Wear suitable protective clothing and footwear.
- Don't prepare food if you are unwell with a tummy bug, or a cough or cold, as you could spread bacteria on to food.

## Clothing and footwear

As a food worker, you must wear clean protective clothing. Your own clothes can bring bacteria into the kitchen. The purpose of this protective clothing or uniform is to prevent contamination from your own clothes getting on to the food. Food workers should not wear their protective clothing away from the workplace. Footwear should be non-slip, flat and comfortable, with protective toe caps to prevent injury.

## Handwashing

You should wash your hands:
- before you start any food preparation
- after touching your hair or face
- after using the toilet
- after using a handkerchief or tissue to cough or blow your nose
- after cleaning or putting rubbish into the bin
- after handling raw meat, poultry, seafood, vegetables or eggs
- after eating or drinking.

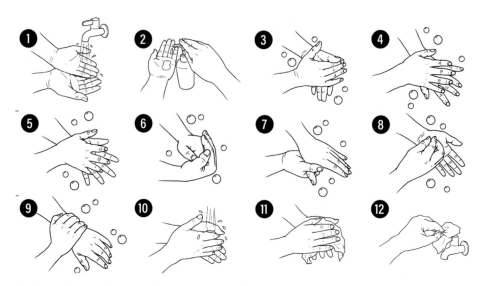

▲ **How to wash your hands properly**

Your nails should be kept short and you should not wear nail varnish when preparing food as it may flake off into the food. Gel, acrylic and false nails are also unacceptable.

## Food worker contamination

▲ **To avoid contamination, use tongs to pick up food**

Food workers can avoid contaminating food by:
- using tongs or wearing gloves to pick up food
- using a clean spoon to taste food when cooking, and avoiding 'double dipping'
- avoiding licking fingers when preparing food
- using the handles when picking up cutlery, and handling just the edges of crockery for food service.

## Pest contamination

**Pests** include flies, insects, birds, mice and rats; they should be kept out of the kitchen and food storage areas.

> **Key term**
>
> **Pests** potentially destructive insects or animals (for example flies, insects, birds, mice, rats)

# Kitchen hygiene

Kitchens should be organised and kept clean so that they are free from bacteria that may cause food poisoning. Work surfaces should be cleaned before, during and after any food preparation. Work surfaces should be cleaned with hot, soapy water, using a clean cloth. An antibacterial spray may be used afterwards; this will destroy virtually all the bacteria on work surfaces. Antibacterial sprays should be used only after the work surface has been cleaned with hot, soapy water, as they kill bacteria but are not designed to remove dirt and grease. Alternatively, a **sanitiser** may be used; this is a cleaning chemical that both cleans and destroys bacteria.

### Key term

**Sanitiser** a cleaning chemical that both cleans and destroys bacteria

## Work surfaces and equipment contamination

Work surfaces and equipment can become contaminated with bacteria from raw foods and unwashed hands. For these reasons, you should always:

- wash your hands before beginning any food preparation
- clean work surfaces before you begin any food preparation
- wash equipment very carefully after it has been in contact with raw meat, poultry, raw eggs, shellfish, fish, pulses and rice
- use clean dishcloths and tea towels every day, or disposable cloths
- use a sanitiser to clean and reduce bacteria to a safe level on work surfaces.

## Colour-coded chopping boards

Different-coloured nylon chopping boards are to be used for different preparation tasks:

- a **green** board is used for salad and fruit
- a **brown** board is used for vegetables
- a **red** board is used for raw meat and chicken
- a **blue** board is used for fish
- a **yellow** board is used for cooked meat
- a **white** board is used for bread and dairy products
- a **purple** board is used for products containing allergens.

▲ Colour-coded chopping boards

### Activity

Here is the menu for a summer barbecue:

- pork sausages
- vegetable kebabs
- chicken drumsticks
- green salad
- bread rolls
- lemon cheesecake.

State which of these dishes could cause food poisoning if not prepared or cooked correctly.

### Extension activity

Describe how the chef in charge of the kitchen would ensure that the food is prepared safely to prevent contamination and food poisoning.

# Washing dishes

Utensils, crockery and cutlery should be washed as soon as possible after use. This cleaning may be done by hand or using a dishwasher. Using a dishwasher has several advantages: the water temperatures can be very hot without the risk of scalding; the process is automated so no stages of the washing and rinsing cycle can be left out; finally, the process is much quicker than hand washing.

## Washing dishes by hand

When washing dishes by hand it is ideal to have two sinks, one for washing and rinsing and a second for sanitising. If you do not have two sinks, washing and rinsing with very hot water can be carried out in the same sink, or you may wash in the sink and rinse in a separate bowl of hot water. The water temperature should ideally be more than 60°C for washing and 80°C for sanitising. These temperatures are very hot, so rubber gloves would need to be used. Alternatively, a chemical sanitiser may be used instead of water at 80°C. The rinsing water should be changed often to ensure it is clean and hot. Rinsing is important as dishes that are not rinsed are still covered with large numbers of bacteria.

# Storing food

- Frozen food should be stored in the freezer at −18°C or below.
- Chilled/high-risk food should be stored in the fridge at 0° to below 5°C.
- Store cupboard ingredients such as flour, unopened jars and cans should be stored at ambient temperature, approximately 17–20°C (this is also known as room temperature).

Stock should be rotated to make sure it is not kept for too long. For more information on stock rotation, see page 107. All foods should be date coded, including foods prepared by the food business itself. Date codes on food should be checked daily.

Ready-to-eat foods and raw foods should not come into contact with each other. They should either be kept in separate fridges or freezers, or ready-to-eat food should be stored above raw food in the fridge or freezer.

Foods with a 'best before' date may be consumed after this date, but the quality may not be as good. Foods with a 'use by' date should be consumed by this date as these foods could cause food poisoning if consumed after this date.

It is important that some raw foods, such as meat, fish, cheese, and ready-to-eat foods such as yoghurts, pies, pasties and cream, are kept out of the temperature danger zone of 5–63°C as in this temperature range bacteria can grow. As a general rule, foods such as these should be kept either very hot, above 63°C, or very cold, below 5°C.

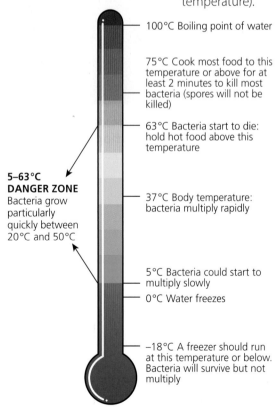

100°C Boiling point of water

75°C Cook most food to this temperature or above for at least 2 minutes to kill most bacteria (spores will not be killed)

63°C Bacteria start to die: hold hot food above this temperature

**5–63°C DANGER ZONE** Bacteria grow particularly quickly between 20°C and 50°C

37°C Body temperature: bacteria multiply rapidly

5°C Bacteria could start to multiply slowly

0°C Water freezes

−18°C A freezer should run at this temperature or below. Bacteria will survive but not multiply

▲ **Key temperatures in food safety**

# Preparing food

Food that is being prepared should be out of the fridge for as short a time as possible. There should be a separate area or, if this is not possible, a temporary clean area for preparing ready-to-eat food. There should be separate colour-coded equipment (for example chopping boards, containers, knives, tongs and utensils) for ready-to-eat foods; alternatively, a dishwasher (or another suitable method of heat disinfection) should be used to clean and disinfect equipment if colour-coded equipment is not available.

Wrapping and packing materials for use with ready-to-eat foods should be stored in the clean area and used correctly. Food workers who handle ready-to-eat food should not handle raw food unless they wash their hands carefully between the two. Fruits and vegetables may be contaminated with bacteria from the soil and should therefore be trimmed and washed thoroughly before serving. Disposable gloves or tongs should be used where appropriate to ensure food is handled as little as possible.

# High-risk foods

**High-risk foods** are also called ready-to-eat foods. They are usually high in protein and moisture, with a neutral pH, which means food-poisoning bacteria can easily grow on them. High-risk foods are eaten without further cooking, so any bacteria that grow on them are not destroyed by heating.

Examples of high-risk foods are:
- cooked meat and poultry
- cooked meat products, such as gravy, soup and stock
- milk and eggs, and the dishes made from them
- shellfish, such as mussels and crabs
- cooked rice.

**Key term**

**High-risk foods (ready-to-eat foods)** these are usually high in protein and moisture, with a neutral pH

# Cooking food

Food should be cooked to an inside temperature of 75°C or hotter to make sure food-poisoning bacteria are killed. (For more information on temperature control, see page 103.) You can check this with a clean temperature probe (use an antibacterial wipe to clean the probe first), which should be inserted into the thickest part of the food. Meat and poultry may be turned during cooking to help them cook more evenly (for example kebabs).

Food should be checked visually to see if it is cooked. For example:
- chicken juices should run clear
- sausages and burgers should be cooked through to the middle, with no pink or red in the centre
- shellfish, such as prawns, should have changed colour and texture; mussels and clams should have open shells
- dishes such as cottage pie, lasagne and curries should be piping hot at 75°C or above.

## Cooling food

If food is not going to be eaten straight away, it may be cooled so it can be eaten cold or reheated later. It is important that food is cooled quickly to make sure it is not in the temperature danger zone for too long, as this will allow bacteria to multiply. Food should be cooled to 8°C or below within 90 minutes. It is possible to speed up cooling time by using a blast chiller, which is a machine used in commercial kitchens that cools food quickly by moving very cold air around the food.

## Serving food

Food may be kept above fridge temperatures (above 8°C) as long as this is for a single period of up to four hours. This is why buffet food may be laid out at room temperature for customers to eat. After this time, it should be thrown away if not eaten, or chilled and kept at the chilled temperature until eaten. It is very important not to display food in this way more than once, otherwise bacteria may grow in the food and cause food poisoning.

**Hot holding** is the term used to describe food being kept hot and ready to serve. Hot food on display should be kept at 63°C or above for no more than two hours. Clean equipment, such as tongs or spoons, should be used to serve ready-to-eat foods. Handling food with the bare hands should be avoided if possible, as this is the main way that bacteria are passed on to food.

> **Key term**
>
> **Hot holding** the term used to describe food being kept hot and ready to serve

## Reheating food

When food is reheated this should be to a core temperature of 75°C. Food should be reheated once only and any leftover reheated food should be thrown away. This is because the food will have passed through the temperature danger zone several times and could cause food poisoning if kept and reheated again.

---

**Activity**

Fill in the gaps with the correct temperatures:
1. Food should be stored in a refrigerator at a temperature of _°C.
2. Food should be stored in a freezer at a temperature of _°C.
3. Food should be reheated to a core temperature of _°C.
4. Hot food on display should be kept at a temperature of _°C.
5. High-risk foods should be kept out of the temperature danger zone of _°C to _°C.

**Extension activity**

Explain why temperature control is so important in storing, preparing and cooking food.

---

# Use of equipment

Fridges and freezers must be operating at the correct temperatures. If food needs to be chilled quickly then a blast chiller can be used.

General rules for using equipment in a kitchen are:

- bins should have lids
- equipment must be washed and disinfected between uses
- disposable gloves or tongs should be used to ensure food is handled as little as possible
- when using equipment, take care to follow the safety instructions for use
- oven gloves should always be used when putting food in the oven and taking it out
- take care that pan handles are always pointing inwards.

## Knives

General rules for using knives include:

- Always clean knives after use to avoid cross-contamination.
- Make sure knives are kept sharp; this causes fewer accidents.
- Use the right-sized knife for the food you are cutting.
- Always store knives carefully, in a block or wrap.
- When carrying a knife, always hold it by the handle with the point facing downwards.

## Knowledge check

1 State three personal hygiene rules.
2 Which coloured chopping boards would you use to prepare the following foods for a chicken and vegetable curry?
   a slicing raw chicken
   b chopping raw onions, carrots, garlic and mushrooms
   c slicing fresh pineapple

3 Why is it good practice to use colour-coded boards when preparing different foods?
4 State the correct temperature of:
   a a fridge
   b a freezer
5 State three safety rules you should follow when handling a knife.

**Activity**

In groups, follow the instructions for heating a ready meal (for example, a lasagne) on the packaging. After heating, use a temperature probe to take the core temperature of the food, to check it is at 75°C or above. If the meal has not reached the correct temperature after the time indicated, note how much longer the food needed to be heated for. Eat the meal. (Don't burn your mouth!)

## Case study

Amy's Bakery is a small, family-run bakery that sells bread and cakes. It uses dairy products and eggs when making cakes, and has developed a successful HACCP system for the bread and cakes it already sells.

The bakery is looking to expand and is considering selling ready-to-eat sandwiches, meat pies and pasties. Two of the sandwiches it wants to make are prawn mayonnaise and egg and cress. Prawns and eggs are high-risk foods and present a potential risk to customers, so the bakery needs to be aware of any potential hazards. The family are not sure about the bakery's expansion into pie and pasty making because they are concerned about using raw meat in their kitchen.

### Questions

1 What advice would you give Amy's Bakery about how to ensure its prawn and egg sandwiches are of the highest quality and safe to eat?
2 Create a production plan, including health, hygiene and safety points, for making prawn mayonnaise and egg and cress sandwiches.
3 Advise Amy's Bakery on whether it should make meat pies and pasties, and consider how much work would be involved in terms of hygiene and safety.
4 Create a production plan for either a prawn sandwich or a chicken and mushroom slice.

# 2.4 Evaluating cooking skills

**What will I learn?**

In this topic you will gain knowledge and understanding of the following areas:

2.4.1   Reviewing of dishes

2.4.2   Reviewing own performance

> **Getting started**
>
> List which parts of your practical assessment you think will need to be reviewed.

## 2.4.1 Reviewing of dishes

Your evaluation should include a brief review of planning, preparation and cooking, highlighting areas of success and areas for potential further development.

When reviewing your dishes, the following areas should be considered.

## Dish production

You will need to review how well you produced each dish. For example, did the dishes turn out exactly as planned or were there any changes that needed to be made?

## Dish selection

You will need to review how suitable your dishes were for the tasks set, and justify why you made the choices you did. For example, if the task set was to make dishes suitable for a ten-year-old child, did your dishes meet the nutritional needs of the child?

## Health and safety

You will need to review how you ensured that your dishes were prepared taking into account health and safety requirements. You will need to consider safe use of equipment, utensils and work area. Think about the following questions.
- Did you use oven gloves?
- How did you use knives safely?

## Hygiene

You will need to review how you ensured that your dishes were prepared taking into account hygiene requirements. You will need to consider your personal hygiene, temperature control, the correct storage of food and the requirements of the Food Safety Act.

Think about:

- using antibacterial soap and spray
- washing hands correctly
- keeping high-risk foods in the fridge
- ensuring foods such as chicken are cooked thoroughly.

## Improvements

You will need to review how you could improve the outcome of your dishes. You can consider all aspects of your dishes, for example improving presentation, colour, flavour, texture and additional accompaniments. You can also consider nutritional value: is it a healthy dish? Does it meet the nutritional needs of the intended customers?

## Organoleptic

Organoleptic (as we have seen on page 149) refers to the use of the sense organs to assess the qualities of foods. This can be done via a **sensory evaluation**. A sensory evaluation will judge:

- appearance
- taste texture/mouthfeel
- consistency
- smell or aroma.

A sensory evaluation will also make sure that your dish meets the customer's expectations.

Table 2.12 **Sensory evaluation word bank**

| Appearance – what the food looks like | Texture – how it feels in the mouth | Taste/smell/flavour |
|---|---|---|
| appetising | chewy | acidic |
| colourful | crispy | bitter |
| dry | crumbly | bland |
| flat | crunchy | buttery |
| golden | doughy | creamy |
| lumpy | dry | fruity |
| risen | gooey | herby |
| shiny | greasy | meaty |
| slimy | hard | salty |
| smooth | juicy | sharp |
| soggy | powdery | sour |
| stringy | rubbery | tasteless |
| syrupy | sticky | tangy |
| thick | spongy | undercooked |
| watery | tender | watery |

When you carry out a sensory evaluation on the dishes you have made, you should use the correct **sensory descriptors**. These are words that describe the appearance, taste and texture of food. The word bank presented in Table 2.12 gives some examples of words used when evaluating food; some words can fit under more than one heading.

There are a number of different ways in which you can carry out a taste test on your dishes.

# Preference test – hedonic ranking

Hedonic ranking is where the tester is asked whether they like or dislike a product. A scale from 'like extremely' to 'dislike extremely' is used to rank the food.

# Profiling test – star profile

This test is used to obtain a detailed description of a food product. Qualities such as mouthfeel, appearance, aroma, flavour and texture are assessed. The results of profiling tests are plotted on a star diagram, and this test is also known as a star profile.

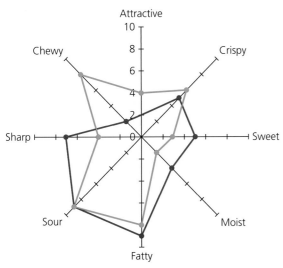

▲ **Star profile of lemon chicken**

Carrying out a taste test will make it easier to evaluate the organoleptic properties of your dish as it will give you an indication of customer acceptance.

**Activity**

What sensory descriptors would you use to describe the following food items?
1  An apple
2  A piece of milk chocolate
3  A raw spring onion
4  A bread roll

# Presentation

A chef would want to present the food they cook to the highest possible standard. This will need to be thought out before the evaluation as part of your review. Think about:

- decoration and garnish of the finished product
- the size and shape of the plates, bowls or dishes used
- extra enhancements to the table (for example a tablecloth and any table decoration, such as flowers or the menu)
- the balance of the food on the plate; consider how much of the food is needed on the plate and the positioning of the food on the plate
- the presentation skills you used (for example piping, latticing, fluting, icing, drizzles).

## Activity

1 Find a picture of each of the following dishes:
   - chicken korma and pilau rice
   - chocolate roulade
   - strawberry pavlova
   - meatballs in a tomato sauce.
2 Stick the pictures in your workbook and write an explanation of why each dish looks attractive.

### Extension activity

Describe how you would present each of the dishes to make it look attractive to customers.

# Waste

In order to be cost-effective there should be little, if any, wastage when preparing your dishes.

You will need to review your management of ingredients used and explain how you ensured that no ingredients were thrown away. Think about:

- buying the exact quantity needed
- weighing and measuring accurately
- if there was any wastage, whether there are any ways in which the waste could be reused
- using a peeler to remove as little skin as possible
- how to achieve correct portion control.

# 2.4.2 Reviewing own performance

This section should consist of a review that identifies your personal strengths and weaknesses relating to:

- decision making
- organisation
- planning
- time management.

When reviewing your own personal strengths and weaknesses, it is always useful to consider WWW (what went well) and EBI (even better if).

## Decision making

You will need to review all the decisions you made throughout the task. Think about the decisions you made regarding:

- factors affecting the planning of your menu
- your production plan
- how you prepared and made your dishes, and the skills used
- presentation techniques
- food safety practices.

## Organisation

You will need to review how well organised you have been throughout the task. Review what you did to ensure you were always organised. Think about:

- what you did to ensure you had the correct ingredients
- how you knew how to make each dish
- what you did throughout the task to keep on track.

## Planning

You will need to review how you planned your menu and how you ensured your chosen dishes matched what the task set was asking you to do. What were the advantages and disadvantages of the dishes you chose to make? Are your dishes suitable for the specific needs of the customer?

## Time management

You will need to review how well you used your time. For example, did you take too long over some tasks? Did your dishes take the right time to prepare and cook? Did you find that you had time to spare, or were you unable to finish on time? You may have chosen the correct dishes and finished on time.

Think about:

- what you did to ensure you used your time effectively
- whether you practised your dishes so you knew timings would work.

## Assignment practice

### Assignment brief

Hill End Farm Shop is located in the countryside. It is only three miles from a small town. A popular footpath route for walkers runs alongside the farm shop. It is situated off a lane, which is also a popular cycle route.

Hill End Farm Shop sells seasonal vegetables and fruit, which are grown on the farm, and supplies beef, pork and chicken that has been reared on the farm. The shop sells eggs from its own chickens, and supplies cheese and milk that have been produced on a nearby dairy farm. The owner has made small quantities of bread, preserves and cakes, which have been very popular and have sold well.

Due to the success of the farm shop, the owners have just renovated a small barn alongside it and are opening a café. The café opening hours are going to be 9 a.m. to 5 p.m., and the plan is to serve breakfast, lunch and afternoon tea, plus separate items to be served with hot or cold drinks. The main customers in the farm shop are older adults who enjoy walking or cycling.

The business likes to use produce grown on its own farm, or to source local ingredients wherever possible. It has a small kitchen with a range of handheld equipment and small electrical equipment, and a large freezer and fridge. It has a large convection oven, and a grill and hob space.

You have been appointed as a commis chef to plan, prepare, cook, present and review two dishes. These dishes can be suitable for breakfast, hot or cold light lunches, afternoon tea, or as individual items to be served with a hot or cold drink. The two dishes must meet the nutritional needs and wants of adult cyclists and walkers.

### Tasks

#### The importance of nutrition (12 marks)

1  Analyse the assignment brief. What are the important factors to be taken into consideration?
2  Recommend two dishes for the café.
3  Assess how the dishes meet the nutritional needs of the customers.
   a  Show an understanding of the importance of the macronutrients and micronutrients.
   b  Explain the impact of cooking methods on the nutritional value of your chosen dishes.

It is recommended you spend 3 hours on this task.

#### Menu planning (18 marks)

1  Discuss the factors that affected your choice of dishes. These may include:
   ■ cost
   ■ portion control
   ■ balanced diets
   ■ time of day
   ■ clients/customers
   ■ equipment available
   ■ skills of the chef
   ■ time available
   ■ environmental issues
   ■ time of year
   ■ organoleptic.
2  Write a production plan for making your two dishes and any accompaniments. Your plan should include:
   ■ commodity list with quantities
   ■ equipment list (including small and electrical equipment)
   ■ health, safety and hygiene
   ■ contingencies (a backup plan in case anything should go wrong)
   ■ quality points
   ■ sequencing and dovetailing
   ■ timings (identify how long each task is going to take, including washing-up and cooking time)
   ■ mis en place (for example collecting equipment and ingredients, checking the recipe and method, weighing and measuring, preparing commodities)
   ■ cooking (temperatures and timings)
   ■ cooling
   ■ hot holding
   ■ serving
   ■ storage.

It is recommended you spend 1 hour on this task.

#### The techniques of preparation, cooking and presentation of dishes (66 marks)

1  Follow your production plan to prepare, cook and serve your dishes, showing that you are following the correct food safety and hygiene

practices. Your teacher will observe you as you do this.

a   Demonstrate how to work safely, following the correct food safety and hygiene practices and procedures when you prepare and cook your dishes and use equipment and facilities.

b   Prepare the dishes, demonstrating a variety of basic, medium and complex knife preparation techniques.

c   Cook the dishes, demonstrating a variety of basic, medium and complex cooking techniques.

d   Present the dishes in a way that is appropriate for the brief.

2   You should demonstrate techniques including:
   - creativity
   - garnish and decoration
   - accurate portion control
   - accompaniments.

It is recommended that you spend 3.5 hours on this task.

## Evaluating cooking techniques (total 24 marks)

1   Assess the production of the presented dishes. Review your planning, preparation and cooking, making sure that you review areas of success (WWW – what went well) and for potential further development (EBI – even better if). Your review should include information on the following.
   - Dish production and selection: How well did you produce each dish? Did the dishes turn out exactly as planned? If you did this assignment again would you do anything differently? Did your dishes meet the brief?
   - Organoleptic: How did you rate your dishes in terms of flavour, aroma, texture and appearance?
   - Improvements: How you could improve the finished results? Consider presentation, colour, flavour, texture and additional accompaniments. You can also consider nutritional value: Is it a healthy dish? Does it meet the nutritional needs of the intended customers?
   - Presentation: What decorations and garnishes did you use and why? What size

and shape of plates, bowls or dishes did you use and why? Did you put any extra enhancements on the table to set the scene? (Think about where the food would be served.)
   - How did you ensure the balance of the food on the plate? How much of the food is needed on the plate? What is the positioning of the food on the plate? What presentation skills did you use and why?
   - Health, safety and hygiene: What did you do to ensure that you took into account all of the health and safety requirements? What did you do to make sure all the food was prepared and cooked hygienically?
   - Food waste: How did you ensure that there was the minimum amount of waste?

2   Review your own personal strengths and weaknesses. Think about WWW (what went well) – your strengths, and EBI (even better if) – your weaknesses. You should include information on the following.
   - Decision making: Consider all the decisions you had to make. What were the best decisions and what decisions were not as successful?
   - Organisation: How organised were you? What aspects of your organisation could you improve?
   - Planning: How did you plan your menu to ensure your chosen dishes matched what the brief was asking you to do? Do the dishes suit a café situated next door to a farm shop in a rural location? What were the advantages and disadvantages of the dishes you chose to make? Were your dishes suitable for the specific needs of the customer (mainly older adults who enjoy walking or cycling)?
   - Time management: What did you do to ensure you used your time effectively? Did you practise your dishes so you knew the timings would work? Did you take too long over some tasks? Did your dishes take the right time to prepare and cook? Did you find that you had time to spare, or were you unable to finish on time?

It is recommended that you spend 2.5 hours on this task.

# GLOSSARY

**Absorption** when digested nutrients are absorbed into the bloodstream

**Aeration** adding air to a mixture by beating or whisking it vigorously

**Allergen** a substance (for example food) that causes an allergic reaction

**Allergy** a food allergy is when a person's body reacts in a negative way to a food they have eaten

**Ambient temperature** normal room temperature

**Amino acid** the basic component of all proteins

**Anaerobic** a process that does not require oxygen

**Angina** when the blood supply to the heart is restricted

**Antibacterial spray** a spray designed to destroy most bacteria on work surfaces

**Appetising** appealing to the senses

**Apprenticeship** a combination of on-the-job training and classroom learning

**Bacteria** single-celled micro-organisms; some types of bacteria can cause food poisoning

**Baking blind** precooking pastry before a filling is added

**Baking** cooking food in a hot oven without adding extra fat during the cooking process

**Barracks** where people in the armed forces live

**Basal metabolic rate (BMR)** how many calories you need to stay alive for 24 hours when warm and resting

**Basting** spooning over stock or fat during cooking to stop food from drying out and to help it to brown

**Bâton** a vegetable cut, also called jardinière, where vegetables are cut into baton shapes

**Beating** combining ingredients together thoroughly

**Beverage** a drink other than water

**Blanching** when food is cooked very quickly in boiling water then cooled to stop the cooking process

**Blending** mixing two or more ingredients together

**Boarders** students who live in school during term time

**Boiling** cooking food in boiling water or other liquid to make it tender

**Braising** a moist method of cooking used for larger pieces of food, when the food is only half covered with a liquid and cooked slowly for a long time at a low temperature

**Breach of legislation** breaking the law

**Brunoise** cutting vegetables into tiny dice from julienne strips

**Budgeting skills** managing money by prioritising essential spending before optional spending

**Calorie** a unit used to measure the energy in food

**Caramelising** cooking sugar until it becomes a deep golden colour

**Catering** providing food and drink services to customers

**Chiffonade** a rolling, slicing action to cut soft, delicate foods such as lettuce and green vegetables such as cabbage into ribbons

**Chilled (fridge) temperature** temperature of 0° to below 5°C

**Chilling** keeping food cool to prevent the growth of harmful bacteria by placing it in a fridge

**Chlorophyll** a green pigment in plants that they need to absorb energy from light for photosynthesis

**Chopping** cutting food into small pieces of roughly the same size

**Commodity** a food ingredient from a plant or animal

**Communal** shared, for example a communal kitchen

**Competition** another business that provides a similar product or service to the same target customers

**Components of dishes** ingredients already combined together; they can be purchased like this (for example ready-made pastry) or to be partly prepared by the chef (for example washed and drained salad ready for use)

**Condemned food** food that is unfit for human consumption

**Confectionery** sweets and chocolate

**Conference** an event where people meet to discuss a particular topic or come together for some training

**Constipation** a condition where emptying the bowels is difficult

**Contingency** a backup plan you can put into place if things go wrong

**Contract** a formal document designed to protect both employee and employer

**Control** a way of reducing the risk of a hazard causing harm

**Cooling** reducing the temperature of food

**Corrective action** an intervention designed to solve a problem

**Creaming** beating ingredients together to incorporate air

**Crimping** pressing a decorative pattern into the edge of a pie crust before it is baked

**Critical control points** points in a food production system where hazards need to be removed or reduced to a safe level

**Critical limits** upper and lower acceptable limits, for example a fridge temperature should be between 0°C and below 5°C (8°C is the legal maximum)

**Cross-contamination** bacteria spreading on to food from a different place, for example hands, work surfaces or utensils

**Debone** removing the bones from a joint of meat, poultry or fish

**Decorations** additions to sweet dishes to make them look more attractive; decorations are not always edible (for example sparklers or candles on a cake)

**Deep fat frying** cooking by immersing small, tender pieces of food in very hot fat for a short time

**Deglazing** loosening the browned juices on the bottom of a pan by adding a liquid to the hot pan and stirring as the liquid boils

**Dehydrating** (of food) removing the moisture from food, for example drying it at a low temperature, to preserve it

**Dehydration** (of people) when the body loses more water than it takes in

**Demographics** information about the population of an area, such as people's age, gender and income

**Deseeding** removing seeds before use

**Dicing** cutting fruit or vegetables into small cube shapes

**Dietary fibre** a type of carbohydrate found in the cell walls of vegetables, fruits, pulses and cereal grains; also known as non-starch polysaccharide (NSP)

**Dietary needs** the requirements of a specific or restricted diet

**Discrimination** the unjust treatment of people, especially on the grounds of race, age or sex

**Disposable income** the money left over for saving or spending after taxes have been subtracted from income

**Dovetailing** preparing part of one dish and then part of another dish before the first dish is finished

**Dress code** a set of rules specifying the type of clothing to be worn

**Due diligence** reasonable precautions taken to ensure that a business complies with the law

**Emulsifying** the process by which two liquids that would not normally mix are mixed together to form an emulsion

**Enforcement action** action required by law following an inspection by an EHO

**Environmental Health Officer (EHO)** council official responsible for inspecting premises involved in food production to ensure that health and safety hazards are minimised

**Equality** being equal, especially in terms of status, rights or opportunities

**Ethical** good or morally correct (for example behaviour)

**Farm to fork** a strategy that allows food to be traced through all stages of production back to the original source

**Fat-soluble vitamins** vitamins that dissolve in fat; these are vitamins A and D

**FIFO** first in, first out policy used to ensure that older stock is used up first

**Fillet** a cut of fish or meat that is free from bones

**Filleting** removing bones (for example the breast from a chicken or the bones from a fish)

**Fixed costs** costs that are constant (for example rent and energy bills) as opposed to other, fluctuating business expenses

**Fluting** pressing a decorative pattern into the edge of a pie crust before it is baked (sometimes called crimping)

**Folding** stirring a whisked or beaten mixture very gently to retain as much air as possible

**Food intolerance** a sensitivity to some foods that can make it difficult for someone to digest them and cause negative side effects

**Food miles** the distance that food is transported as it travels from producer to consumer

**Food safety management system** practical steps to identify and control hazards in order to establish and maintain food safety

**Fortified cereals** cereals with added vitamins and minerals

**Free sugars** sugars that are added to food (they are not part of the cell wall of a plant)

**Freezer temperature** temperature of −18°C or below

**Freezing** storing food at a temperature of −18°C or colder

**Front of house** the part of the hospitality and catering business where employees have direct face-to-face contact with customers

**Frying** a fast method of cooking using a small amount of fat to cook food in a frying pan

**Gap in the market** an unmet consumer demand

**Garnishes** edible decorations on savoury food dishes

**Gelatinisation** occurs when starches such as cornflour are heated with a liquid, thickening the liquid

**Gelation** when a thickened mixture is chilled and then set

**Glamping** camping that offers more luxurious facilities than traditional camping

**Glazing** making a shiny surface on food to give it an attractive appearance

**Grating** producing coarse or fine threads by repeatedly rubbing a food on one of the sides of a grater

**Greenhouse gases** the gases that trap heat and raise the Earth's temperature (for example carbon dioxide, methane, nitrous oxide)

**Griddling** cooking over heat using a chargrill or griddle pan

**Grilling** a dry method of cooking food by applying heat to its surface

**Gross profit** the amount of money remaining when the cost of goods sold (food and drink in this case) has been deducted

**Growth spurt** a rapid increase in height

**Haemoglobin** part of the red blood cell that carries oxygen around the body

**Halal** something that is permitted under Islamic law, for example particular foods and methods of preparing them

**Hazard analysis** analysis that aims to identify the stages in the food production process that could cause harm to the consumer

**Hazard Analysis and Critical Control Points (HACCP)** a system for identifying and controlling hazards within a food business

**Hazard** something that could cause harm

**Hazardous** risky or dangerous

**Health and Safety Executive (HSE)** a UK government agency responsible for the enforcement and regulation of workplace health, safety and welfare

**Health and safety policy statement** a written statement by an employer of its commitment to health and safety for its employees and the public

**Heart attack** when the blood supply to the heart is cut off

**Heart palpitation** a noticeably rapid, strong or irregular heartbeat

**High biological value protein** a protein that contains all of the essential amino acids

**High blood pressure** a higher than normal force of blood pushing against the arteries

**High-risk foods** (ready-to-eat foods) these are usually high in protein and moisture, with a neutral pH

**Hospitality** providing accommodation, food and drinks in a variety of places outside the home

**Hot holding** the term used to describe food being kept hot and ready to serve

**Hydrating** adding water to an ingredient, which is then absorbed by the ingredient

**Immune system** the processes of the body that protect against disease

**In the field** when members of the armed forces are away from their base camp

**Ingest** take (food, drink or another substance) into the body by swallowing or absorbing it

**Internal organs** the organs inside the body, such as the heart, lungs and kidneys

**Invoice** bill sent to someone for goods or services they have received

**Juicing** extracting the juice from fruits or vegetables

**Julienne** cutting vegetables into matchstick-shaped strips

**Kitchen brigade** the team of people who work in the kitchen, with each one having a clear role

**Kneading** pushing, pulling and folding bread dough until it becomes smooth and silky

**Kosher** food that is permitted under Jewish dietary laws

**Lacto-ovo vegetarians** vegetarians who eat no fish, meat or meat products, but eat eggs and dairy foods

**Lacto-vegetarians** vegetarians who eat no fish, meat, meat products or eggs, but eat dairy products such as cheese and milk

**Laminating** (pastry) folding and rolling dough to create very thin layers that will trap air

**Layering** placing different foods on top of one another to create an attractive combination

**Lifestyle** how someone chooses to live and what they like to do

**Low biological value protein** a protein that lacks one or more of the essential amino acids

**Loyalty scheme** a scheme set up by a retailer to monitor buying habits and to retain customers by giving incentives (for example money-off vouchers)

**Marinating** soaking a food in a marinade to help develop its flavour, tenderise it and, in some instances, colour it before it is cooked

**Mashing** reducing a food to a soft mass using a masher or ricer

**Measuring** assessing the volume/amount of ingredients

**Melting** using heat to change a solid ingredient into a liquid

**Melting using a bain-marie** melting an ingredient over hot water

**Menstruation** when a person has a monthly period

**Mess** an area where people in the armed forces eat and socialise

**Mincing** reducing food to very small pieces

**Mise en place** the preparation of dishes and ingredients before starting to cook

**Mixing** the process of combining two or more ingredients to become one

**Mobility problems** when someone has problems moving around

**Monitoring** observing, watching, checking

**Net profit** the money remaining when all costs (material, labour and overheads) have been deducted from sales income

**Neutral foods** foods with a pH of around 7

**Non-perishable foods** foods with a longer shelf life (for example breakfast cereals), which are usually kept at room temperature

**Obese** very overweight

**Organoleptic** involving the use of the sense organs, for example to assess the qualities of food

**Pasteurisation** the process of prolonging the keeping quality of products such as milk by heating it to 72°C for 15 seconds to destroy harmful bacteria

**Pathogenic** harmful bacteria that can cause food poisoning

**Peeling** removing a thin layer of the skin of fruit and vegetables using a peeler or knife

**Perishable foods** foods with a shorter shelf life (for example fresh meat), which are usually stored in the fridge

**Personal attribute** a quality or characteristic that a person has

**Personal protective equipment (PPE)** clothing or equipment designed to protect the wearer from injury

**Pescatarians** people who eat no meat or meat products, but eat eggs, fish and dairy foods

**Pests** potentially destructive insects or animals (for example flies, insects, birds, mice, rats)

**Physical activity level (PAL)** the amount of physical activity you do each day, for example sitting, standing, running and exercise

**Pickling** preserving foods in an acidic solution such as vinegar

**Piping** pressing a soft food through a piping bag fitted with a shaped nozzle to form the food into an interesting shape

**Poaching** cooking food in a liquid that is just below boiling point

**Pro rata** proportional/proportionally; how much you are paid depends on how many hours you work

**Profit** the amount of money remaining when costs have been deducted

**Proving** leaving a dough, such as bread, to rise before baking

**Pulses** the collective term for peas, beans and lentils

**Puréeing** making a food into a smooth mixture

**Ramadan** a month in the year when Muslims fast from dawn to sunset

**Ready-to-eat foods** foods that require no further cooking or reheating

**Reduction** simmering liquid over heat so that the water content evaporates, resulting in a concentrated liquid

**Risk assessment** a way of identifying things that could cause harm to people in the workplace

**Risk** how likely it is that someone could be harmed by a hazard

**Roasting** cooking and browning with the aid of fat

**Rolling** spreading out or flattening

**Room service** food ordered and delivered to your room in an establishment such as a hotel

**Rub-in** using the fingertips to combine ingredients, for example rubbing fat into flour to make pastry

**Safer food, better business (SFBB)** an example of a food safety management system

**Salary** a fixed payment from an employer to an employee per set period, for example monthly or annually

**Sanitiser** a cleaning chemical that both cleans and destroys bacteria

**Sautéing** cooking food quickly in fat

**Scissor snipping** using scissors to cut a food such as chives into small pieces

**Searing** cooking the outside of meat quickly on a high heat to form a crust and keep the meat juices inside

**Segmenting** dividing a food such as an orange or grapefruit into pieces

**Seizing** if water gets into chocolate when it is melting it can 'seize', becoming grainy and unusable

**Sensory evaluation** judging food based on its appearance, taste, aroma and texture

**Sensory descriptors** words to describe the appearance, taste, aroma and texture of food

**Sequencing** preparing and cooking dishes in a suitable order so that they are ready to serve on time

## Glossary

**Setting** when a liquid becomes firmer

**Shaping** modelling food to create an attractive form

**Shelf life** how long a food product lasts for before it starts to go bad

**Shredding** slicing into long thin strips

**Sieving** passing an ingredient through a wire or plastic mesh sieve

**Skimming** removing excess fat and impurities (for example from a stock) using a slotted spoon

**Skinning** removing the skin from a food

**Slicing** cutting a thin or broad piece from a larger piece of food (for example a slice of bread) or cutting a wedge-shaped piece of food from a larger circular piece (for example a slice of pizza)

**Spatchcock** to split a small chicken, or any other bird, in half by removing the backbone so it is flattened; it can then be barbecued or grilled

**Split shift** a shift that is split into two parts, for example lunchtime and evening

**Spore** a dormant form of bacteria able to survive when food storage conditions are not ideal

**Starchy foods** foods high in starch, such as pasta, rice, potatoes and bread

**Steaming** cooking food in the steam produced by boiling water

**Stir-frying** a quick method of cooking, where small pieces of food are fast-fried in a small amount of oil in a wok

**Stock** all materials, ingredients and equipment used

**Stock rotation** the practice of using the product with the shortest shelf life before using a similar one with a longer shelf life

**Sugary foods** foods high in sugar, such as jam, cakes, biscuits and ice cream

**Temperature danger zone** the temperature range at which bacteria can grow, between 5°C and 63°C

**Temperature probe** a device used to check the internal temperature of food

**Tempering** heating then cooling chocolate to a specific temperature so that when it cools it has a glossy surface and will break with a sharp snap

**Tenderising** when the tough muscle fibres in meat or poultry are broken down in order to make the meat more tender to eat

**Toasting** cooking or browning food using direct heat, such as a grill, toaster or open fire

**Toque** the traditional tall, white, pleated chef's hat

**Toxin** a poison, especially one produced by micro-organisms such as bacteria

**Trimming** removing the visible fat from meat, or excess pastry

**Unmoulding** turning a food out of a mould

**Variable costs** costs that change (vary) depending on the amount of business an establishment does, for example amount of stock purchased

**VAT** a tax added to goods and services; the standard rate is currently 20 per cent

**Vegans** vegans eat a completely plant-based diet, containing no food of animal origin or products containing ingredients derived from animals, so no meat, fish or eggs, and no dairy products

**Vulnerable groups** groups of people who are more at risk of health issues, for example the very old and the very young

**Wage** money paid by an employer to an employee in exchange for work done; usually an hourly rate

**Water bath (sous-vide)** a method of cooking food, especially meat or fish, by vacuum-sealing and immersing in warm water then cooking very slowly

**Weighing** measuring ingredients by weight

**Whisking** (aeration) when a food is beaten vigorously to trap air into it

**Wok** a rounded frying pan

**Workflow** in the front of house, the flow of food and drinks from the catering kitchen and bar to customers in the dining areas, bars or lounges

**Zesting** removing the coloured outer skin of citrus fruits

# ACKNOWLEDGEMENTS

I would like to thank my family and friends for their continued support and encouragement throughout the writing process.

Bev

My thanks, as always, to my family and friends; especially Katie, Rency and Sofie from Gems Wellington International School.

Yvonne

## Photo credits

## AcknowledgementS

© Ratmaner/stock.adobe.com, b l-r © Exclusive-design/stock.adobe.com, © Exclusive-design/stock.adobe.com, © JoannaTkaczuk/stock.adobe.com; p. 122 t l-r © Nickola_Che/stock.adobe.com, © Ievgen Skrypko/stock.adobe.com, © Laplateresca/stock.adobe.com, vitamin C © Markus Mainka/stock.adobe.com, calcium © Photocrew/stock.adobe.com, b © Bit24/stock.adobe.com; p. 123 t © Yaruniv-Studio/stock.adobe.com, b © Yulia Furman/stock.adobe.com; p. 124 © Anaumenko/stock.adobe.com; p. 125 t © Pololia/stock.adobe.com, b © Fahrwasser/stock.adobe.com; p. 126 © Viktor Kochetkov/stock.adobe.com; p. 127 © Pixel-Shot/stock.adobe.com; p. 128 © Monkey Business Images/Shutterstock.com; p. 129 © Nyul/stock.adobe.com; p. 134 t © StockImageFactory/stock.adobe.com, b © NewFabrika/stock.adobe.com; p. 135 © The Vegetarian Society; p. 136 The Vegan Trademark is owned by the Vegan Society; p. 138 t-b © Tuayai/stock.adobe.com, © Africa Studio/stock.adobe.com, © Cagkan/stock.adobe.com; p. 139 t-b © Kostiantyn Zapylaiev/123 RF.com; © Jelena990/stock.adobe.com, © Africa Studio/stock.adobe.com, © Evan Sklar/Alamy Stock Photo, © Andrey Armyagov/stock.adobe.com, © Lulu/stock.adobe.com; p. 142 © Dusk/stock.adobe.com; p. 143 t © Macqua/stock.adobe.com, b, Public Health England in association with the Welsh Government, Food Standards Scotland and the Food Standards Agency in Northern Ireland, © Crown copyright; p. 144 © Arenaphotouk/stock.adobe.com; p. 149 © Steve/stock.adobe.com; p. 153 © The British Egg Information Service; p. 159 © Kucherav/stock.adobe.com; p. 160 © Mdbildes/stock.adobe.com; p. 161 © NewAfrica/stock.adobe.com; p. 162 © Kkolosov/stock.adobe.com; p. 163 © Ecummings00/stock.adobe.com; p. 164 © Prostock-studio/stock.adobe.com; p. 165 © Martin Lee/stock.adobe.com; p. 166 © Africa Studio/stock.adobe.com; p. 167 © Ruslans Golenkovs/stock.adobe.com; p. 168 l © Nikodash - iStock via Thinkstock/Getty Images, r © Sergejs Rahunoks - 123RF; p. 169 © Plprod/stock.adobe.com; p. 170 t © Ffolas/stock.adobe.com, b freefoodphotos.com under Creative Commons Licence; p. 171 t © Andrew Callaghan, b © Stanislav Goncharuk/stock.adobe.com; p. 172 t © Christophe Fouquin/stock.adobe.com, b © Andrew Callaghan; p. 173 t © Andrew Callaghan, b © Станислав Гончарук/stock.adobe.com; p. 174 © Inats/stock.adobe.com; p. 176 © Monkey Business/stock.adobe.com; p. 179 t © Schankz/stock.adobe.com, b © New Africa/stock.adobe.com; p. 181 t © Dmytro Smaglov/stock.adobe.com, b © Amandaliza/iStock/Thinkstock/Getty Images; p. 182 t © Stephen/stock.adobe.com, b © Sarahdoow/stock.adobe.com; p. 185 © Vanessa tan/EyeEm/stock.adobe.com; p. 186 t © Vladimirkolens/stock.adobe.com, b © Philip/stock.adobe.com; p. 187 t © Zzayko/stock.adobe.com, b © FomaA/stock.adobe.com; p. 188 © Pvstory/stock.adobe.com; p. 189 © andesign101/stock.adobe.com; p. 190 © Pkheawtasang/stock.adobe.com; p. 191 © Yay Images/stock.adobe.com; p. 192 © AmalliaEka/stock.adobe.com; p. 193 © Psd photography/stock.adobe.com; p. 196 t © CoolFinger101/stock.adobe.com, b © Funny face/stock.adobe.com; p. 197 © DJC/Alamy Stock Photo

# INDEX

# Index

# Index

ovens 44
overheads 33
overweight 128, 132
paper towels 47
part-time work 27, 29
pasteurisation 90, 91
pastry 164–6, 169, 182
pay, rates of 29, 30
payment systems 36–7
peak times 31–2
peanut allergies 86
peeling 169
pensions 30
people skills 25
performance reviews 207, 209
perishable foods 94, 103, 105–7
personal attributes 24–5
personal hygiene 195–6, 203–4
personal protective clothing 112
Personal Protective Equipment at Work
    Regulations (PPER) 1992 69
pescatarians 136
pest contamination 196
photosynthesis 120
physical activity level (PAL) 129–30
pickling 180
pilafs 178
piping 166, 185
planning skills 207, 209
plant-based foods 147
plastics 62
plate service 9, 14
plating techniques 188–9
poaching 139, 183
pods 3–4
poisoning 91
    see also food poisoning
portion control 142, 192–3
potassium 123, 124
poultry 43, 105, 107, 171–3
pound, value of the 34
preference tests 205
pregnancy 128
preparing food 102–9, 158–84, 199
    techniques 158–68, 208–9
presentation techniques 146, 185–94,
    206, 208–9
preservation methods 180
price of food 142
prisons 11
pro rata 29
processed foods 105
production planning 152–6
profiling tests 205
profit 141, 142, 144
    gross/net 33
promotion 37–8
protein 58, 119–20, 127–8, 136–7
proving 161

public health 110
public houses (pubs) 9
pulses 135
punctuality 25
puréeing 164
qualifications 26–8
quality points 153
quantity lists 152
quenelles 186
radio 38
Ramadan 134
rashes 99, 100
Rastafarians (Rastafarianism) 134–5
raw foods 105, 153, 198–9
ready-to-eat foods 101–3, 198–200, 202
    see also high-risk foods
reception 41
receptionists 21
record-keeping 73, 75, 78–80, 106–7
recycling 36, 147
red blood cells 124, 126–7, 129, 133
reduce philosophy 35, 147
reduction 180
refreshments 16
regulations, food safety 97–8
reheating food 103, 200
religious beliefs 59, 130, 134–5
remuneration 30–1
Reporting of Injuries, Diseases and
    Dangerous Occurrences Regulations
    (RIDDOR) 2013 70, 73
residential services 2–5, 11, 15–17
restaurants 9–10, 18, 41
    pop-up 9, 63
reuse philosophy 36, 147
rewards 31
ribbons 190
rice, braised (pilafs) 178
risk assessment 67–8, 70–3, 75, 113
risks 70–1, 80–1, 112
roasting 139, 180
rolling 164
room service 5, 16
room types 15
rub-in 164
safer food, better business (SFBB) 79–80
safety materials 47
salaries 30
Salmonella 90, 99, 153
salt 95–6, 133
sandwiches 81
sanitisers 47, 197
sauces 189
sautéing 180
schools 13, 27
scissor snipping 190
scoops 192–3
scoring with a fork 190
searing 180

seasonality 29, 31–2, 35, 62, 148
security risks 70–3
seeds 86, 165, 177
segmenting 174
seizing 166
self-catering 53
sensory descriptors 205
sensory evaluation 204
sequencing 153
service charges 31
serving food 13–15, 59, 102–9, 155, 200
sesame seeds 86
setting 180
shallow-frying 139
shaping 167, 186
shared facilities 15
sharing economy 19
shelf life 105, 106
shredding 161
sickness pay 30
side dishes 193
sieving 161
Sikhs (Sikhism) 135
silver service 14
skills 25, 145–6
skimming 177
skinning 165
slicing 171
smartphones 37
social media 38, 60–1
sodium 124
soya allergies 86
spas 17
spatchcock 171
special dietary needs 129–37, 130, 145–6
split shifts 29
spores 88, 91
stadia 8
staffing levels 31–2
Staphylococcus aureus 90
star profiles 205
star ratings 17
starches 120, 127, 180
steamers 46
steaming 139, 180–1
stenciling 187
stir-frying 139, 181
stock 49
stock control systems 49, 107
stock rotation 45, 107, 141, 198
storing food 94, 106–7, 155–6, 198
Stradey Park Hotel 57
street-food trucks 8
stroke 132
success 33–9
sugar 95–6, 120, 128, 133
    free 133
    work 190
suites 15